Language, Madness, and Desire

MICHEL FOUCAULT

LANGUAGE, MADNESS, AND DESIRE

On Literature

Edited by Philippe Artières, Jean-François Bert,
Mathieu Potte-Bonneville, and Judith Revel

Translated by Robert Bononno

UNIVERSITY OF MINNESOTA PRESS

MINNEAPOLIS

LONDON

Originally published in French as *La grande étrangère: À propos de littérature,* by Michel Foucault. Copyright 2013 by Éditions de l'École des Hautes Études en Sciences Sociales.

Selections of poetry from "Simulacre," "Le Point cardinal," "Glossaire j'y serre mes gloses," "Bagatelles végétales," and "Marrons sculptés pour Miró" are reprinted from *Mots sans mémoires,* by Michel Leiris. Copyright 1969 Éditions Gallimard, Paris.

English translation copyright 2015 by Robert Bononno

Published by the University of Minnesota Press
111 Third Avenue South, Suite 290
Minneapolis, MN 55401–2520
http://www.upress.umn.edu

LIBRARY OF CONGRESS CATALOGING-IN-PUBLICATION DATA
Foucault, Michel, 1926–1984.
Language, madness, and desire: on literature / Michel Foucault; edited by Philippe Artières, Jean-François Bert, Mathieu Potte-Bonneville, and Judith Revel; translated by Robert Bononno.
ISBN 978-0-8166-9323-8 (hc)
1. Literature—History and criticism. I. Artières, Philippe. II. Bert, Jean-François. III. Potte-Bonneville, Mathieu. IV. Revel, Judith. V. Bononno, Robert, translator. VI. Title.
PN45.F5913 2015
801—dc23   2015005045

Printed in the United States of America on acid-free paper

The University of Minnesota is an equal-opportunity educator and employer.

21 20 19 18 17 16 15   10 9 8 7 6 5 4 3 2 1

Contents

IIIIIIIIIIIIIIIIIIIIIIIIIIIIIIIIIIIIIIIIIIIIIIIIIIIIIIIIIIIIIIIIIIIIIIIIIIIIIIIIIIIIIIIIIIIIIIIIIIIIIIIIIIIIIIIIIIIIIIIIIIIIIIIIIIIIII

Editors' Introduction

"At one time, I read a great deal of what is referred to as 'literature.' In the end, I rejected many of them because of inability, most likely because I didn't have the right code to read them. Now [1975] we have books such as *Under the Volcano* and *The Opposing Shore*. A writer I like very much is Jean Demelier; I was very impressed with *Le rêve de Job*. Tony Duvert's work as well. For those of my generation, great literature was American literature, it was Faulkner. It's reasonable to assume that having access to contemporary literature through foreign literature alone, whose source one can never reach, introduces a kind of distance with respect to literature. Literature was the great unknown."[1]

In this 1975 interview about Jacques Almira's *Le voyage à Naucratis* (the manuscript of which he received in the mail), Michel Foucault indulged in a rare description of the literature in his library.[2] As we can see, this short list is very diverse. The range of Foucault's readings extended from young authors like Jean Demelier[3] and Jacques Almira to Julien Gracq. At the same time, he expressed his admiration for Thomas Mann, Malcolm Lowry, and William Faulkner,[4] an admiration that, in 1970, led him to visit Faulkner's world, traveling the Mississippi River valley all the way to Natchez. Foucault's history as a reader has yet to be fully explored. According to his brother, in their childhood home in Poitou, two separate libraries confronted one another: one was paternal—learned, medical, and off limits—and resided in the office of his father, a surgeon; the other was maternal, literary, and open. There, Foucault discovered Balzac, Flaubert, and classical literature. At school, where he was educated by members of the Catholic clergy, he read Greek and Latin.[5] It was on the Rue d'Ulm, where he had access to the amazing library of the

École Normale Supérieure, one of the leading public libraries in France, which held poetry and philosophical treatises, critical essays and historical texts, that Foucault was able to experience a form of unrestricted reading. In the ENS library, maintained by Maurice Boulez, he deconstructed an order of discourse, and literature appeared before his eyes.[6] Daniel Defert, in his chronology in *Dits et écrits,* provides some additional information: Foucault read Saint-John Perse in 1950, Kafka in 1951, Bataille and Blanchot in 1953, followed the progress of the *nouveau roman* (including the work of Alain Robbe-Grillet), discovered Raymond Roussel in the summer of 1957, the authors associated with *Tel Quel* (Philippe Sollers, Claude Ollier) in 1963, reread Becket in January 1968.

We cannot overlook the importance of Foucault's foreign travels in 1956: daily trips to the archives of the Maison de France in Uppsala and the Centre de civilisation française in Warsaw had a significant effect on Foucault's close relationship to literary language. Amid the solitude of the Swedish and Polish winter, Foucault read a great deal—René Char's poetry was his bedtime reading—and taught literature. It was there, surrounded by two languages that were foreign to him, that he underwent his first great experience with writing, there too that he taught French several hours a week and several courses on French literature, including a memorable lecture on love in French literature from Sade to Genet. In Sweden, Foucault led a theater club, where he put on several contemporary works with his students.[7] In 1959, in Cracow and Gdansk, he gave lectures on Apollinaire. More anecdotal evidence in the history of Foucault the reader is found in his meetings, while in Uppsala, with Claude Simon, Roland Barthes, and Albert Camus, who had come to receive the Nobel Prize. Just as, toward the end of his life, he frequented several young writers (Mathieu Lindon, Hervé Guibert) without ever "discussing" literature, it is likely that he read these authors without ever entering into a dialogue with them, just as he never met Maurice Blanchot, claiming that "he admired him too much to become friends with him."[8] During the early 1960s, Foucault engaged in an intimacy with literature that is apparent from an examination of his preparatory notes for the *History of Madness*. An investigation of the archives of institutionalization, registers from Bicêtre, as well as *lettres de cachet* served initially as a literary experience, which he would later describe to the historian Arlette Farge in the introduction to *Le désordre des familles*.[9] Foucault was drawn to the beauty of the poetics of the archive — pure graphic existences — which he himself referred to as "the course that literature would follow from the seventeenth century onward."[10]

Nonetheless, he continued to guard himself against such intimacy. For example, Foucault describes his first encounter with the work of Raymond Roussel, an author to whom he devoted an entire book in 1963, as follows: At the José Corti bookstore, "I found my attention drawn to a series of books of that faded yellow color used by publishing firms of the late nineteenth century . . . I came upon the work of someone I had never heard of named Raymond Roussel, and the book was entitled *La Vue*. Well, from the first line I was completely taken by the beauty of the style."[11]

The "great unknown" would, in fact, be a clandestine moment; for Foucault was not just a demanding reader and a writer whose style, with the release of each of his books, came to be admired and recognized. Reading him closely, at a time when we have access not only to his major publications but also to his collected writings *(Dits et écrits)* and his lectures at the Collège de France, it has become clear that the philosopher's relationship with literature—the documents contained in the present volume are a magnificent testimony to this—was complex, critical, and strategic.

In reading the many prefaces, interviews, and lectures that Foucault devoted to literature in the 1960s (whether they address writers such as Blanchot and Bataille directly or examine the traditional units of literary criticism in terms of a critique of the author or a general description of the space of language), and in recalling that these texts not only form an insistent counterpoint to the great "archaeological" works but reveal, even within those works, a discrete echo through their references to Orestes or *Rameau's Nephew (The History of Madness),* to Sade *(Birth of the Clinic),* or to Cervantes *(The Order of Things),* we obtain a better grasp of the singularity of this concern for the literary. Although it forms an integral part of the attitude of an entire generation and prolongs an insistent component of French thought that consists in treating fiction and poetry as touchstones of the philosophical act (a standard against which Bachelard, Sartre, and Merleau-Ponty are successively measured), Foucault's concern takes the form of an intensification of his own discourse. An intensification or, rather, a permanent doubling, that is to say, tentative, extreme, expressing both the order of the world and its representations at a given moment (which we know of, from the development of Foucault's research, as the archaeological description of a "system of thought") and what, paradoxically, would represent, in spite of everything, the dimension of excess, the immoderate, the *outside.* Where the great early works, notwithstanding the variations in their specific object (madness, the clinic, the birth of the social sciences), analyzed just how much our way of organizing discourse about the world owed to a series of historically determined divisions, the texts on literature, which are contemporary with them, appear, on the contrary, to employ an entire range of strange figures—intransigent writers, frozen words, labyrinths of writing—that embodied, if not an explicit refusal, at least a notable exception. Only once do the "orientation of the books" and that of Foucault's literary texts overlap. This occurs in *Death and the Labyrinth,*[12] his book on Raymond Roussel, the only work in which historical and epistemic inquiry appear to have completely disappeared, to be reformulated, indirectly, in terms of precisely that which brings about the failure of the order of discourse: a gesture, no doubt—that of writing—but also something that immediately implies a way of using literature as a strategy. Throughout this period Foucault is led to simultaneously maintain, to bring into play both the non-specificity of literature and its opposite, its strategic centrality. In the first case—that of archaeological inquiry—literature possesses no specificity in comparison with other discursive productions (official documents, treatises, excerpts from archives, encyclopedias, scholarly works, private letters, journals); in the second ("literary" texts), it is a question of expressing, within literature itself, a relationship between a posture and procedures of writing that, because they appear in a particular form, engender something like an experience of dis-order, the realization of a rupture: a matrix of change, an operator of metamorphosis. In short, the implacable correlation of words and things, on the one hand, and this strange finding, on the other, that what can be said is sometimes impossible to think—a strange disjunction that introduces an entire field of experimentation in which discourse could also free itself of its own codes or the unequivocality of what it presents to the reader: "Roussel's enigma is that each element of his language is caught up in an indenumerable series of contingent configurations. A secret much more manifest but also much more difficult than that suggested by Breton: it does not reside in a ruse of meaning or in the play of unveilings but in a *concerted incertitude of morphology,* or perhaps in the certitude that a *variety of constructions can articulate the same text,* authorizing incompatible but mutually possible systems of reading—*a rigorous and uncontrollable polyvalence of forms.*"[13]

Two remarks can be made about this. On the one hand, this "outside" that literature represents for Foucault with regard to his own analyses is inseparable from an intentional gesture. It is not literature as such that is invested with this vertiginous *polyvalence of forms,* the downward motion of our order of the world toward the gulf of its own confusion, but the gesture that bears it along: literature as strategy, that is to say, a certain *use of literature,* the implementation of *procedures,* and the work of internally destroying the economy of narrative, which involves the construction of a battlefield against the hegemony of meaning. On the other hand, this "outside" exceeds the definition Blanchot had given it and that Foucault himself had used beginning in the mid-sixties. This was the acknowledgment of the dissolution of the link between "I think" and "I speak," the unrestricted seepage of language outside itself. It is also, immediately, the establishment of another mode of being of discourse, one that escapes the dynasty of representation and engages material processes for constructing those structurally resistant words, which, depending on the situation, can be: inaudible, scandalous, unclassifiable, untranslatable, undecidable, fragmentary, aleatory, inconstant, vertiginous.

By the end of the 1960s, this strange relationship to literature seemed to dissipate. There are, no doubt, many reasons for this; but there are three that bear commenting on. The first has to do primarily with the abandonment of the privilege of the discursive over other forms of practice. The order of discourse is an order (historically determined) of the world; it is one of the modalities through which we organize our relationship to things, to ourselves, and to others, but it does not represent an exclusive model. Occasionally, a discursive order precedes and establishes other divisions (for example, the birth of an institution, a type of physical procedure, social exclusion), sometimes it even seems to be the result. Similarly, the "disorder" of a certain use of literature is one attempt among others to fracture the order of the world, for there are other strategies, speech not mediated by writing being one example. But there are also ways of "guiding one's own behavior" that serve as so many strategies of rupture, of questioning, or of overturning the order of the world. From this point of view, the gradual abandonment of the field of literature as a "duplication" of Foucault's own research can be attributed to the desire to extend his inquiry to broader themes—this time presented in terms of power and resistance. Literary writing, used as an engine of war, can certainly find its place here, but it no longer represents the paradigm.

The second pertains to the difficulty of justifying a decision. We spoke of the *uses* of the literary and *procedures of writing*: this requires will, for it entails a project. Yet the old idea—no doubt still replete with phenomenological reminiscences—according to which it is around the intersection of literature and madness that speech capable of "unhinging" language is wound, makes the problem of a project hard to discern. What then can we say about the *will* of someone like Louis Wolfson[14] or Jean-Pierre Brisset?[15] And even when this will is made explicit, what of Foucault's increasing interest, beginning in the early 1970s—and, especially, following that other experience with speech represented by his involvement with the Groupe d'information sur les prisons (GIP)—with the transition to a collective dimension? How can we connect "dis-order" (whether it involves the deconstruction of the linguistic code, the questioning of an institution, or the refusal of the objectification of his own identity) to shared practices integral not only to a unique subjectivity but to nonhierarchical subjectivations? Here, we find a renewed questioning of the elimination of certain "literary cases" from the established order and a much more general inquiry into the political modalities of the resistance involved: from this point of view, the muffled roar of battle is anything but a *literary* metaphor.

And finally, the third pertains to the abandonment of the figure of the "outside," explicitly recognized by Foucault (the outside is a myth), and the reinvestment of the notion of the difference possible inside history—inside relationships of power, inside words spoken and endured, broken images and those that, in spite of everything, we continue to reproduce. The question then becomes one of how we might, from within a certain epistemic and historical configuration, from within the "network of the real" deployed by a certain economy of discourse and practice at a given moment—in short, from within a grammar of the world as historically determined—unearth and reverse connections, shift lines, move points, hollow out meaning, and reinvent equilibria. The stakes are, of course, theoretical, but they are also, immediately, political. Can we, from within this history, which makes us what we are (that is, think the way we think, speak the way we speak, act the way we act), free ourselves of those determinations and paradoxically establish the space (always internal) of a *different* speech or way of life? It is this problem, very clearly revealed throughout his work on literature, that will now continue to haunt Foucault: the possible overcoming and historical determination of what we are must be conceived not in terms of a contradiction, but in terms of compossibility. We are very distant, here, from the transgression so important to Bataille or the Blanchotian *outside.*

Foucault's comments about literature, which compose the present volume, fall within this perspective; they share a common feature that makes their presence in the "Audiography" series hardly accidental. All are oral commentaries made over a period of less than ten years—between 1963 and 1971—but each of them maintains a particular relationship to writing and language. The first two documents are complete transcriptions of radio broadcasts that were made on French radio in January 1963. During the broadcasts, Foucault read several excerpts from texts by Shakespeare, Cervantes, Diderot, Sade, Artaud, Leiris, and others.

The second group consists of two lectures on "Literature and Language" given in Brussels in December 1964, while the third is a long, unpublished typescript for a two-part essay presented in 1971 at the University of Buffalo. This was part of an oral experiment (conducted on at least three occasions) for a study of the Marquis de Sade for which the manuscripts have been preserved. Bringing them together in this way, it is not the irony of a subjectless language trying to find expression or that of a form of neutral writing constrained to become speech that we would like to present; on the contrary, returned to the written page, they contain elements of a polymorphous uneasiness with exteriority, materiality, and the ruses of discourse, an uneasiness for which Foucault, reluctant to claim authorship, became, for a while, the mouthpiece.

Note on the Text

||||||||||||||||||||||||||||||||||||||||||||||||||||||||||||||||||||||||||||||||||||||||||||||||||||||||||||||||||||||||||

This book is based on typed transcriptions of oral presentations given by Michel Foucault in the form of radio broadcasts or lectures. The versions presented here are the most literal possible, but the transition from the spoken to the printed word imposes certain editorial interventions. Errors or inaccuracies in the transcription have been corrected or completed based on the manuscripts Foucault used to prepare his oral presentations. Punctuation and paragraph breaks have, in some cases, been altered to improve readability, although we made every effort to comply with Foucault's intentions. Illegible words in a typed or handwritten manuscript are indicated in the text by the editors.

The critical apparatus in the notes is limited to a discussion of manuscript variants whenever it was felt these were significant or where there were breaks in the typescript. We have also included bibliographic and biographical information about authors who might be unfamiliar to readers.

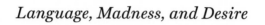

Language, Madness, and Desire

Language and Madness

In 1963 Michel Foucault gave five talks on the subject of language and madness for a radio program known as *The Use of Speech,* which was broadcast nationally by RTF France III. Jean Doat, an actor and writer with a background in theater and television, was the producer. These five broadcasts, presented once a week over a period of five weeks, were titled "Celebratory Madness" (January 7, 1963), "The Silence of the Mad" (January 14, 1963), "Persecution" (January 21, 1963), "The Body and Its Doubles" (January 28, 1963), and "Mad Language" (February 4, 1963). The series of talks given by Foucault was introduced as follows:

Michel Foucault, in writing the history of Western societies, has used madness as his touchstone. Every society, every culture, assigns madness a very specific place, preparing a defined structure for it in advance; thus, the group of so-called reasonable men is defined in opposition to the mad on the basis of its proscriptions.

This series of broadcasts contains four segments. In the first, the author defines the points where madness erupts into language. He analyzes the different forms of pathological language. He presents texts written by patients and read by actors, as well as recordings of dialogues between patients and clinicians.

In the second part, Michel Foucault shows how madness has been represented in language. He examines the character of the madman in Shakespeare and Corneille (the character of Éraste in *Mélite, or The False Letters*).

In the third part, Foucault describes the experience of madness within language itself and exposes certain links between the literary experience and madness among writers such as Gérard de Nerval and Raymond Roussel. Roussel was treated by the great psychopathologist Pierre Janet, who describes Roussel's case in one of his works, where he is given the name Martial.[1]

Finally, Foucault discusses artificially provoked madness, and no one could better illustrate this last aspect of language and madness than Henri Michaux.

In this volume, we present "The Silence of the Mad" and "Mad Language," the second and last broadcasts, because of the mirror structure they employ and their focus on literature. The other three broadcasts are largely devoted to the single question of the language of the mad. When Foucault asks the actors to read passages from literature, no reference is made to the edition from which the texts are taken, which is a potential source of error in the printed reproduction of the spoken text. In the case of foreign literature, where the problem of translation arises, we have made use of the Pléiade editions available at the time Foucault presented his broadcasts, while respecting the cuts made within the text by Foucault, which are here indicated in square brackets.

The Silence of the Mad

||||||||||||||||||||||||||||||||||||||||||||||||||||||||||||||||||||||||||||||||||||||||||||||||||||||||||||||||||||||||||||||||||||||||||||

Jean Doat: Michel Foucault, you have agreed to give a series of talks for our program, *The Use of Speech,* on the language of madness. That's correct, isn't it? The first broadcast in the series took place last week and was called "Madness and Celebration." What's the subject of your second presentation?

Michel Foucault: Well, I'd like to devote today's broadcast to something that concerns the opposite, the other side of celebration, which would be the silence of the mad. But I believe you have an objection to make and I feel we should talk about it because, Jean Doat, you're a man of the theater and are kind enough to produce this broadcast. I have the impression you're not completely in agreement with me about my interpretation of the respective roles of celebration and theater with respect to madness. I have the impression that theater turns its back on celebration, turns its back on madness, that it tries to attenuate their powers, to control their force and subversive violence in favor of the beauty of representation. The theater, ultimately, destroys the participants, the participants of the celebration, to bring to life the actors on one side and the audience on the other. In place of the mask of celebration, which is a mask of communication, it substitutes something made of cardboard or plaster, something more subtle but which conceals and separates.

J.D.: Well, I can tell you that it's not a strictly personal opinion. I believe, along with many others, especially with good master Alain,[1] that the theater was born from a community's need to express itself to itself. As it gradually perfected itself, part of that community became professionalized and became known as authors, actors, set designers, and all the other professions involved in the presentation, and the other part became known as the audience. But I feel, as Alain—and I'll ask his help on this—still believes, for you two are friends as I understand it, I think that Alain has not forgotten to introduce an element of theater into celebrations and ceremonies. For my part, I feel that the theater is never as beautiful as when it takes place outside the venues created for it. Think of festivals, think of events that take place in certain outdoor settings, in front of cathedrals. Ultimately, I feel that, simply put, there is always a kind of equilibrium to be sought between two forces—Apollonian and Dionysian.

M.F.: And you feel that theater is on the Dionysian side, where I would say that it is on the Apollonian.

J.D.: In reality, I simply feel that the theater, like any art, but more than any other art, is a search for man's transcendence and that man recognizes himself in this character who transcends himself in the theater.

M.F.: Well, look, shall we conduct an experiment? Why don't we listen to a scene from *King Lear,* the great scene of madness in the play, the scene on the heath. Maybe we can examine this and let the listeners judge for themselves.

> *Lear.* Blow, winds, and crack your cheeks! rage! blow!
> You cataracts and hurricanes, spout
> Till you have drench'd the steeples, drown'd the cocks!
> You sulphurous and thought-executing fires,
> Vaunt-couriers of oak-cleaving thunderbolts,
> Singe my white head! And thou, all-shaking thunder,
> Strike flat thick rotundity o' the world!
> Crack nature's molds, all germins spill at once
> That make ingrateful man!
> *Fool.* O nuncle, court holy-water in a dry house is better
>   than this rain-water out o' door. Good nuncle, in, ask thy

daughters' blessing: here's a night pities neither wise man
nor fools.

Lear. Rumble thy bellyful! Spit, fire! spout, rain.
Nor rain, wind, thunder, fire, are my daughters:
I tax not you, you elements, with unkindness;
I never gave you kingdom, call'd you children,
You owe me no subscription: then let fall
Your horrible pleasure; here I stand, your slave,
A poor, infirm, weak, and despised old man:
But yet I call you servile ministers,
That have with two pernicious daughters join'd
Your high-engender'd battles 'gainst a head
So old and white as this. O! O! 'tis foul!

Fool. He that has a house to put's head in has a good head-
piece.

    The cod-piece that will house
      Before the head has any,
    The head and he shall louse
      So beggars marry many.
    The man that makes his toe
      What he his heart should make
    Shall of a corn cry woe,
      And turn his sleep to wake.

For there was never yet fair woman but she made mouths in
a glass.

Lear. No, I will be the pattern of all patience;
I will say nothing.

Enter Kent.

Kent. Who's there?

Fool. Marry, here's grace and a cod-piece; that's a wise man
and a fool.

Kent. Alas, sir, are you here? Things that love night
Love not such nights as these; the wrathful skies
Gallow the very wanderers of the dark,
And make them keep their caves: since I was man,

Such sheets of fire, such bursts of horrid thunder,
Such groans of roaring wind and rain, I never
Remember to have heard: man's nature cannot carry
The affliction nor the fear.
Lear. Let the great gods,
That keep this dreadful pother o'er our heads,
Find out their enemies now. Tremble, thou wretch,
That hast within the undivulged crimes
Unwhipp'd of justice: hide thee, thou bloody hand;
Thou perjured, and thou simular man of virtue
That art incestuous: caitiff, to pieces shake,
That under covert and convenient seeming
Hast practised on man's life: close pent-up guilts,
Rive your concealing continents and cry
These dreadful summoners grace. I am a man
More sinn'd against than sinning.
Kent. Alack, bare-headed!
Gracious my lord, hard by here is a hovel;
Some friendship will it lend you 'gainst the tempest:
Repose you there; while I to this hard house—
More harder than the stones whereof 'tis raised;
Which even but now, demanding after you,
Denied me to come in—return, and force
Their scanted courtesy.
Lear. My wits begin to turn.
Come on, my boy: how dost, my boy? art cold?
I am cold myself. Where is this straw, my fellow?
The art of our necessities is strange,
That can make the vile things precious. Come, your hovel.
Poor fool and knave, I have one part in my heart
That's sorry yet for thee.[2]

It seems to me, Jean, that the scene we've just heard supports both our positions, and there's nothing surprising about this because *King Lear* is, without doubt, the very rare, the very solitary portrayal of a fully and completely tragic expression of madness. It is without equal, without equal in a culture like our own because our culture has always taken care to keep madness at a distance and consider it from a somewhat remote, and always justified, point of view, in spite of the occasional indulgences of comedy.

We already find this small break in the language of Cervantes.

The tragedy of *Don Quixote* does not reside in the madness of the character or the profound strength of his language. The tragedy of *Don Quixote* resides in the small empty space, in that distance, sometimes imperceptible, that allows not only its readers but also other characters, including Sancho and Quixote himself ultimately, to become aware of this madness.

And so, this disturbing and pale glimmer, which offers Quixote insight into his madness at the same time as it pulls it away, is very different from the suffering of Lear, who, from the depths of his madness, knows he's been falling and will continue to fall until the moment of his death. Don Quixote, on the contrary, can always go back, he's always that close to stepping back from his own madness.

So, yes, he's about to become aware and then, in the end, he doesn't, he continues to blind himself and, all the same, there comes a moment when the reversal will take place, but the tragic law of his madness demands that this return, this sudden awareness of his own madness, as if a fever were breaking, results in death and the unavoidable certainty of death.

> [. . .] for whether it was due to the melancholy caused by his defeat or simply the will of heaven, he succumbed to a fever that kept him in bed for six days, during which time he was often visited by his friends the priest, the bachelor, and the barber, while Sancho Panza, his good squire, never left his side. [. . .] the bachelor told him to be of good cheer and to get out of bed so that they could begin the pastoral life, for

which he had already composed an eclogue that would put all those written by Sannazaro to shame, and he said he had bought with his own money two famous dogs to guard the flocks, one named Barcino and the other Butrón, which had been sold to him by a herder from Quintanar. But not even this could bring Don Quixote out of his sorrow. [...]

Don Quixote asked to be left alone because he wanted to sleep for a while. They did as he asked, and he slept more than six hours at a stretch, as they say, so long that his housekeeper and his niece thought he would never open his eyes again. He awoke after the length of time that has been mentioned, and giving a great shout, he said:

"Blessed be Almighty God who has done such great good for me! [...]

My judgment is restored free and clear of the dark shadows of ignorance imposed on it by my grievous and constant reading of detestable books of chivalry. I now recognize their absurdities and deceptions [...] I feel, Niece, that I am about to die; I should like to do so in a manner that would make it clear that my life was not so wicked that I left behind a reputation for being a madman, for although I have been one, I should not like to confirm this truth in my death." [...]

They exchanged glances, astonished by Don Quixote's words and although they had their doubts, they tended to believe him; one of the signs that led them to think he really was dying was how easily he had moved from madness to sanity [...]

In brief, Don Quixote's end came after he had received all the sacraments and had execrated books of chivalry with many effective words. The scribe happened to be present, and he said he had never read in any book of chivalry of a knight errant dying in his bed in so tranquil and Christian a manner as Don Quixote, who, surrounded by the sympathy and tears of those present, gave up the ghost, I mean to say, he died. [...]

This was the end of the Ingenious Gentleman of La Mancha [...]

The tears of Sancho and of Don Quixote's niece and house-keeper, new epitaphs for his grave, are not recorded here, although Sansón Carrasco did write one for him:

> Here lies the mighty Gentleman
> who rose to such heights of valor
> that death itself did not triumph
> over his life with his death.
> He did not esteem the world;
> he was the frightening threat
> to the world, in this respect,
> for it was his great good fortune
> to live a madman, and die sane.[3]

This epitaph, and the entire ending of *Don Quixote,* demonstrate one thing: that madness and the awareness of madness are now like life and death. One destroys the other. Wisdom may very well speak of madness, but it will speak of it as a corpse. As for madness, it will remain silent, the pure object of an amused gaze. Throughout the classical era, madmen were a part of the social landscape, a picturesque social landscape that served at most to reintroduce a skeptical uneasiness: after all, I myself may be mad, but I know nothing about it because madness is not self-aware and since everyone else is mad I have no reference point from which to determine whether or not I'm mad.

But these are one-sided games and the exercises of subtle or devious minds. What interests me in this classical age is a massive fact, a historical fact, but hidden, which has remained silent for a long time. It may not be very important for the history of historians, but for me, it seems to be very important with respect to the history of a culture. So, here it is.

One day in April 1657, nearly six thousand people were arrested in Paris. Six thousand in seventeenth-century Paris, that's nearly a hundredth of the population. It's as if, for example, we were to arrest, in today's Paris, something like forty thousand people. That's a large number and we would hear about it.

They took those people to the Hôpital Général de Paris.[4] Why? Oh, because they were unemployed, they were beggars, they were useless, they were libertines, eccentrics, and they were also homosexuals, madmen, the insane. They were sent to the Hôpital Général although no one, at any time, had taken any specific legal steps against them. A precautionary measure by the police, an order from the king, or even—something more serious from my point of view—a simple request by the family, was sufficient to send all of those good people to the hospital, and for life. Obviously, there was nothing hospital-like about this hospital; it was more like a large prison, where people were held in custody, often for life.

This practice lasted for nearly a century and a half and, from this enormous ritual of exclusion, which was, by the way, rarely questioned, we retain no more than a few dusty record books, currently stored in the Bibliothèque de l'Arsenal. And in those records, what do we see? Well, we find the lengthy rhapsody of the reasons for internment.

I feel they're worth listening to, those decrees that logic, the logic of the state, which is to say, ultimately, the logic of the police, and the logic of everyday people, directed at the madness of others. For example, some of the reasons given for internment for the month of January 1735 include the following:

> January 3, 1735, Catherine Bar is a public prostitute who is causing considerable disorder in her neighborhood.

> January 6, Jean-Pierre Forrestier often falls into a frenzy, for which he was condemned in Rouen to be locked up.

> January 10, Étienne Gaustier is a libertine who cruelly mistreats his wife and is looking for a way to have her murdered.

> January 17, Malbert has been known for a long time as a dangerous subject and troublemaker whose only profession is to sup-

port disreputable places. Recently, he was living with a woman named Labaume and made several attempts to assassinate her husband.

January 19, Tablecourt, has gone insane.

January 19, Antoine François was found to possess goods that he agreed he had stolen from various shopkeepers.

January 24, Joseph Latour Dupont is an angry man who was condemned to be broken for being a murderer and is completely mad.

January 25, Michel Guillotin is a violent man who cruelly mistreats his wife, who broke the furniture, who insults his father and mother, and had them bitten by a big dog.

January 31, Charlotte Laporte is a convulsive.

January 31, Marie-Jeanne Rousseau is mad and without any hope of return.

January 31, Duval is insane.

January 31, Anne Migneron is a servant of Sieur Buquet and pregnant with his child.

January 31, Jean-François Dubos always mistreats his wife, who is ruining him, and whom he has reduced to poverty along with a child. He is given to all sorts of debauchery.

You see the extent to which reason is laconic and imperative when it involves judging its opposite. It did this throughout the classical period. And yet, for anyone willing to listen, we can discern a kind of gentle murmur, as if madness, even during this period of classical rationalism, sought to recompose its language, to rediscover the old Dionysian communion, and it invokes this lost experience, less with words no doubt than with gestures, gestures that expressed the jubilation of its new birth and its anguish at being deprived of speech for so long.

And Diderot, who may have been the most attentive philosopher of the eighteenth century, saw this experience take shape before his eyes, through gesticulation alone, mixed with cries, noises, sounds, tears, laughter, like a kind of great, wordless coat of arms of madness, which is the dance of *Rameau's Nephew*:

Whereupon he began pacing up and down, quietly humming some of the melodies from *L'Isle des Fous*, *Le Peintre amoureux de son modèle*, *Le Maréchal ferrant*, and *La Plaideuse*. From time to time, raising his hands, he'd gaze up at the sky and exclaim: "My God, isn't that beautiful, isn't that beautiful! How could anyone possessing a pair of ears even ask such a question?" Next he started working himself into a passion. He was sighing softly, and as his excitement increased his voice grew louder; then he began gesturing, grimacing, and twisting about. I said to myself: "Right now he's about to lose his head, and there'll be another scene." And indeed, he suddenly shouted: "I am a worthless wretch ... my lord. My lord, permit me to depart ... oh earth, receive my gold; guard my treasure well ... my soul, my soul, my life! Oh earth! ... my dear friend is here ... he's here! ... *aspettare e non venire ... a Zerbine penserete ... Sempre in contrasti con te si sta ...*" Now he was muddling and mixing some thirty airs of every style— Italian, French, tragic, comic; sometimes singing a bass part, he'd descend into the depths of hell; sometimes straining at the notes as he imitated a falsetto, he'd tear at the upper registers, all the while imitating, with gait, carriage, and gestures, the different characters singing; by turns furious, mollified, imperious, derisive. Now he's a young girl in tears, mimicking all her simpering ways; now he's a priest, a king, a tyrant, threatening, commanding, raging; now he's a slave, obeying. He grows calmer, he grieves, he laments, he laughs; never does he misjudge the tone, pace, and meaning of the aria's words and character. All the chess players had abandoned their games and gathered round him. Outside, the windows of the café were thronged with passers-by attracted by the noise. The roars of laughter were loud enough to open cracks in the ceiling. He noticed nothing of this; he just went on with his performance, transported by a passion, an enthusiasm so akin to madness that it wasn't clear whether he'd ever recover from it, or whether he shouldn't be flung into a carriage and taken straight to the madhouse, still singing a fragment from Jommelli's *Lamentations*. He was performing the most beautiful passages of each work with incredible fidelity, sincerity, and warmth: the exquisite, fully orchestrated recitative where the prophet depicts the devastation of Jerusalem he accompanied with a torrent of tears, which drew further tears from the eyes of the onlookers. Everything was there—the delicacy of the melody, the intensity of expression, and the pain. He stressed the moments where the composer had shown himself to be a particularly fine master of his art; if he abandoned the vocal part, it was to take up the instruments, which he'd suddenly drop to return to the voice; connecting one with the other in such a fashion as to preserve the links and the unity of the whole; taking possession of our souls and keeping them suspended in the most extraordinary state of being I have ever known ... Was I filled with admiration? Yes, I was. Was I moved to pity? Yes, I was; but a tinge of ridicule was blended with these feelings, and denatured them.

You'd have burst out laughing, seeing how he imitated the various instruments. The horns and bassoons he did with bulging, ballooning cheeks and a hoarse, mournful tone; for the oboes he adopted a piercing, nasal sound; he speeded up his voice to an unbelievable pace for the stringed instruments, seeking the truest sounds; the piccolos he whistled; the transverse flutes he warbled; shouting, singing, flinging himself about like a madman, being, just he alone, at once dancer and ballerina, tenor and soprano, the entire orchestra, the entire theater, dividing himself into twenty different roles, running and then stopping, with the air of one possessed, eyes flashing, lips foaming. The heat was overpowering; the sweat, mingled with the powder from his hair, was streaming along the creases of his brow and down his cheeks, and flowing in channels over the upper part of his coat.[5]

It seems to me that Diderot's profile of this strange character, this nephew of Rameau, at the end of the eighteenth century, reveals a symmetry with a very different man, namely, Sade.

There's nothing in Sade like Rameau, of course. Sade's discourse is this infinite, meticulous, inexhaustible discourse, rigorously controlled in its smallest details. And I believe we can contrast the pantomime of Rameau's nephew, who is rejected wherever he goes, who is thrown out by his protectors, who roams the streets after dinner, or chasing after clients, and who emphasizes the madness of his gestures, with the symmetrical and opposite figure, the great immobility of Sade. In Sade, who was securely locked up for forty years and never stopped talking, we find the pure discourse of a pure madness, a gestureless madness, without eccentricity, the pure madness of an immoderate heart.

And then Sade's ever-so-reasonable language, so infinitely rational, has reduced our reason, our own reason, to silence or, at least, to embarrassment, to stuttering.

Our reason can no longer exercise its burning passion for giving orders. For example, we have only to experience the discomfort of the unfortunate doctor at Charenton by the name of Royer-Collard, who, appointed to the asylum, to what had just been transformed into an asylum for the mentally ill, discovered someone by the name of Sade.

The man is terrified, at least he's very worried, and he immediately writes to Fouché, the minister of police—the scientist writes to the politician, in other words, reason invokes reason—he writes to tell him that Sade should not be kept in an asylum for the insane because Sade is not mad. Or rather, he's mad, but his madness isn't really madness; or, rather, this madness is worse than madness because it's reasonable and lucid and lucid with a lucidity that contradicts all reason and ultimately ends in madness. Finally, the good Royer-Collard can no longer escape and feels he's at the bottom of an abyss from which we ourselves, perhaps, have yet to escape.

Your Excellency,

I have the honor of appealing to the authority of Your Excellency with regard to a matter that fundamentally affects my functions as well as the good order of the establishment whose medical services I am responsible for. There is a man at Charenton whose bold immorality has unfortunately made him too well known and whose presence in this facility is causing the most serious disturbances: I am speaking of the author of the contemptible novel *Justine.* This man is not mad. His only mania is one of vice and this form of mania cannot be repressed in an institution devoted to the medical treatment of insanity. Such individuals must be subjected to the most severe sequestration, either to protect others from his fury or to isolate him from any objects that might exacerbate or encourage his hideous passion. However, Charenton does not meet either of those two conditions. Monsieur Sade enjoys far too much freedom here. [. . .]

I can only suggest to Your Excellency that a prison or fortress would be much more appropriate for him than an establishment devoted to the treatment of the ill, which requires the most assiduous surveillance and the most delicate moral precautions.

You'll say that this letter from Royer-Collard to Fouché is conventional, ordinary. And it doesn't make much sense. Yet, I feel it does. This letter, with all the contradictions it contains, indicates, it indicates something that, in our culture, had considerable weight. And that is this embarrassment, this embarrassment that has never left us since the nineteenth century, in the face of madness and the language of madness.

This letter ultimately represents the understanding that the madness that had been so carefully delineated, cataloged, and incarcerated at the Hôpital Général can no longer be assigned to a specific place. We no longer know where it comes from or where it's going. It is homeless and amoral.

So, naturally we dream, we dream of a fantastic fortress where we could enclose it forever. That is what the good doctor Royer-Collard would like to see. But we know that this fortress of absolute tranquillity, which would forever reduce madness to silence, does not exist.

Ever since Sade's indefatigable language, a void was created beneath our words, out of which an unforeseen language continuously arises. This is no longer the language of Dionysian communion that was identified and heard in the sixteenth century; it's a much more difficult language, more muffled and muted. A language that stems from and speaks of an absence, an empty world. In Sade this was the emptiness of a desire that was never satisfied. I feel that this, in someone like Artaud, is a kind of central void, the fundamental void where there are no words, where thought is absent from itself, eats away at its own subsistence, collapses into itself. And it is there, in that impossibility of speaking, in that impossibility of thinking, in that impossibility of finding its words that madness, in our culture, rediscovers its sovereign right to language.

Not without a final detour, however. Madness can speak, but on condition that it takes itself as object. That is to say, that it can present itself—one step removed, unlimited to itself, it can very well say "I"—but in a kind of doubled first person. And, here, the correspondence between Antonin Artaud and Jacques Rivière is significant. Rivière had received some poems that Artaud wanted to have published in *La Nouvelle Revue Française*; however, Rivière didn't feel that the poems could be published. So Artaud answered; he wanted his poems to be heard at all costs. And so that they might be heard, he returned to that disintegration of thought out of which those poems arose. And now Rivière, who hadn't heard the poems, now he can hear the explanation given for them, and Artaud's explanation of why it's impossible for him to write poems where he is. And finally, this explanation becomes a document, becomes a pure poem, a second language, maybe a first, and this becomes that extraordinary work, the correspondence between Artaud and Rivière.

June 5, 1923

Dear Sir,

At the risk of troubling you, will you allow me to hark back to some of the terms of this afternoon's conversation.

For the question of the admissibility of these points is a problem which concerns you as much as me. Of course, I am talking about their ultimate acceptance, their literary existence.

I suffer from a fearful mental disease. My thought abandons me at every stage. From the mere fact of thought itself to the external fact of its materialization in words. Words, the forms of phrases, inner directions of thought, the mind's simplest reactions, I am in constant pursuit of my intellectual being. Thus, *when I am able to grasp a form,* however imperfect, I hold on to it, afraid to lose all thought. As I know I do not do myself justice, I suffer from it, but I accept it in fear of complete death.

This is all very badly expressed and risks interjecting a dangerous misunderstanding in your judgment of me.

Therefore, out of respect for the principal feeling which dictates my poems and those keener ideas and expressions I hit upon, I still offer these poems to the world. I felt and accepted these expressions, these poorly written phrases you reproached me for. Remember, I did not question them. They came from the deep insecurity of my thoughts. I am only too happy when this insecurity is not replaced by the complete non-existence I sometimes suffer.

Here, too, I am afraid you will misunderstand me. I

would like you to understand clearly it is not a matter of the sort of partial existence which comes from what is commonly called inspiration, but from total abstraction, from true wastage.

This is also why I told you I had nothing further, no work in the offing, the few things I submitted to you being the vestiges of what I was able to salvage from the utter void. [. . .]

And for my part the question is nothing less than knowing whether or not I have the right to go on thinking, either in prose or poetry.

Antonin Artaud

May 24, 1924

Dear Mr. Artaud,

I have been holding out against an idea which occurred to me and which definitely attracts me. I want you to think about it. I hope it will please you. Besides, it still has to be worked out.

Why not publish one, or all of the letters you wrote me? I have just re-read the one dated 29 January. It is really quite remarkable.

It would only require a little substitution. I mean we could give the writer and his correspondent pen names. Perhaps I could even draft a reply based on the one I sent you, but treated at greater length and more impersonal. We might also add lines of your poetry or some of your essay on Uccello, the whole constituting a rather interesting novel in letters.

Let me know what you think of this.

Yours,
Jacques Rivière

May 25, 1924

Dear Mr. Rivière,

Why lie, why try to put something which is life's very cry

on a literary level? Why fictionalize something made from the soul's ineradicable essence, which is like the complaint of reality? Yes, your idea pleases me, I am delighted with it, it fills me with joy, provided we do not give the reader the impression he thinks he is looking at fabricated work.

We have the right to lie, but not about the heart of things. I do not want to put my name to the letters. But the reader must definitely think he has the elements of a true story in front of him. We would have to publish my letters from the first to the last, going back to June 1923. The reader should have all the facts under discussion in front of him.

Antonin Artaud[6]

And by this final detour, our culture finally developed an ear for this language, which never flagged and unsettles our own. And it did so through this subterranean work of madness in language, against language; the work of madness in recovering its own language; it seems to me that all this subterranean work enables us now to listen with new ears, with the first ear, to this poem by a patient that Mario Ruspoli also heard, one day, in the Hospital of Saint-Alban.[7]

Contrast
snow on the sea
white patches, land crabs
Image
playing cards
colored hourglasses
sheets.
Tapestry in which the characters are generations of the living.
Good, nature creates.
So, I ask to be followed because I've been told I was mad
   because I claim that nature creates. Good. *The Victory of
   Samothrace,* that's why I was told I was mad. It splits the
   sky. Seeing it, it's hard to believe it was fashioned by the
   hand of man, not that man isn't capable of admirable

things but, and I have no idea how I'm so sure, it contains
something that surpasses the works of man. Thus: a stroke,
a line, light, which escapes it and returns, irradiates it.
It was not created, it creates. Yes, that's it. It is outside
everything. Nobody would claim that the Montagne Sainte-
Victoire where Cézanne let his incomparable gaze wander
was his work, but *The Victory of Samothrace* could only
have come from the hand of the gods. A theological blue
confined to the Île-de-France and Beauce. Suddenly the sky
was a sustained blue, a blue found in the miniatures of the
Middle Ages, a blue found in the miniatures of the Duc de
Berry, a theological blue. Where was the hand, the hand, if
you like, of the creator?

And there the poem ended.

Mad Language

IIIIIIIIIIIIIIIIIIIIIIIIIIIIIIIIIIIIIIIIIIIIIIIIIIIIIIIIIIIIIIIIIIIIIIIIIIIIIIIIIIIIIIIIIIIIIIIIIIIIIIIIIIIIIIIIIIIIIIIIII

I believe there's a simple idea that we're all more or less familiar with. We willingly believe that the madman is mad even before he begins to speak and that it's from the depths of this madness, of this originally silent madness, that he allows the obscure words of his delirium to rise up, belatedly in some sense, and circle around him like a swarm of blind flies.

What I've tried to do in these broadcasts, oh, obviously not to show but simply to help convey—and I'd like to let the word *convey* stumble over its multiple meanings—what I've been trying to help convey to the listeners is that between madness and language, the lineage is not straightforward, nor is there any pure line of descent; rather, language and madness are linked, they are part of a tangled and inextricable fabric from which there can ultimately be no separation.

I have the impression, if I can put it this way, that, very fundamentally, within us, the possibility of speaking, the possibility of being mad, are contemporaneous, and like twins they reveal, beneath our steps, the most perilous but also, possibly, the most marvelous or the most insistent of our freedoms.

At bottom, even if everyone in the world were rational, there would always remain the possibility of traversing the world of our signs, the world of our words, our language, of confusing their most familiar meanings, through the sole and miraculous eruption of a handful of colliding words, of turning the world upside down.

Every man who speaks enjoys, at least in secret, the absolute freedom of being mad and, conversely, every man who is mad and seems, by that very fact, to have become absolutely foreign to the language of men is also a prisoner in the closed universe of language.

You're going to say that madness and language might not have been originally so closely connected, and a number of objections could be made. One could very well use as counterexamples the people I spoke about last week, who watched as the great silent images of their delirium spread silently within them, within their bodies, as if it were an aquarium; or the persecuted individuals I spoke of two weeks ago, who felt they were being pursued by some kind of surveillance, by an anonymous gaze, who knew they were being hunted long before they were able to articulate that feeling in a delusional accusation.

Well, we can state one thing, which is that madness, even when it is silent, always passes through language. It may be nothing more than the strange syntax of a form of discourse.

For example, we now know that the persecuted individual who hears voices speaks those voices himself. He has the impression that they are coming from outside him, but in reality, a recording device that we can attach to his larynx is sufficient to prove that he himself spoke those voices. So that the threats he hears and the oaths or complaints with which he responds are never anything more than the phases or, if you prefer, the phrases, of the same verbal matrix.

We also now know that the body, the body itself, is like a language node. Freud, that great listener, clearly understood that our body, much more than our mind, was a wit, that it was a kind of master craftsman of metaphors and took advantage of all the resources, all the richness, all the poverty of our language. We know that in the case of a woman suffering from hysterical paralysis, if she lets herself fall when she is stood upright on her legs, it's because, at the root of her existence, she feels she was destined to collapse ever since the day when someone, as we say, *dropped her.* But she expresses this with her body.

So, if we have difficulty communicating with the insane, maybe it's not because they don't talk but because they talk too much, in a supercharged language, a kind of tropical abundance of signs in which all the pathways of the world are jumbled together.

But a question then arises: why has this language of madness assumed such importance today? Why now, in our culture, is there such strong interest in all those words, in all those incoherent, senseless words, that might possibly embody a much more significant meaning?

I think we could say that, ultimately, we no longer believe in political freedom, and the dream, the famous dream of unalienated man, is now subject to ridicule. So, out of all those illusions, what do we have left? Well, we have the ashes of a handful of words. And what is possible for the rest of us today, what is possible for us, we no longer entrust to things, to men, to History, to institutions, we entrust to signs.

Very roughly, we could say the following: in the nineteenth century we spoke, we wrote to finally free ourselves in a real world where we would have the leisure to remain silent. In the twentieth century, we write—of course, I'm thinking of literary speech—we write for the experience of writing and to evaluate a freedom that no longer exists other than in words, but in those words it has become a mania.

In a world where God is dead once and for all, and where we know, despite the promises from all sides, from the Right and from the Left, that we won't find happiness, language is our only resource, our only source. It reveals to us in the very hollow of our memories and beneath each of our words, beneath each of those words that gallop through our head, it reveals the majestic freedom of being mad. And maybe that's why the experience of madness in our civilization is uniquely acute and forms, in some sense, the woodland limit of our literature.

So, this evening, I would like, if you will, to follow the line of thought we've developed during previous broadcasts. Not to proceed from madness as a language that starts out by moving toward literature but, on the contrary, to speak of the literary language that already lies within the very confines of madness.

I realize that currently there's a considerable amount of somewhat folkloric prestige attached to the literature of the asylum, the literature of the insane. I would like to speak of something else, of this strange literary experience by which language revolves around itself to discover, behind our familiar verbal tapestry, an astonishing law. We could formulate that law as follows: it's not true that language is applied to things so they can be translated; on the contrary, it is things themselves that are contained and enfolded in language, like a buried treasure that lies silently within the roar of the sea.

Words, their arbitrary encounter, their confusion, all their protoplasmic transformations are sufficient in themselves to bring into being a world that is both true and fantastic, a world much older than our childhood, whose moving grasses Michel Leiris has so aptly captured in *Scratches*:

> When I was told there had been a fire at Billancourt, at first I didn't really understand. *Billancourt,* a name that trailed over the skylights, the weathervanes, and the courtyards like smoke from a factory, like the squeaking of a tram rolling along its rails, and whose three syllables knocked against one another sadly the way the few thick sous collected by a beggar chink together in the bottom of the wooden bowl that he shakes in the hope of exciting the compassion of the heedless people. *À Billancourt*—what immediately struck me most about these syllables was their clean tonality, and I transformed them into these three words: *habillé en cour.* It wasn't a question of a court costume—of this I was always convinced: both Louis XIV and Queen Ranavalo had very little to do with what came trailing along with the name *Billancourt.* If it was a question of dressing in court dress, this clothing could not have anything at all in common with fancy ball dress, the kind of outfit you put on to go parading down

galleries reflected many times over in mirrors, or through enclosed verandas with doors wide open in search of a breeze that isn't there, when black statues draped in gaudy fabric melt into the water. To be in court dress was to be dressed in a way that was comfortable for running fast, for using maximum speed to get to places where people were shouting "*au feu!*" [fire!] or "*au secours!*" [help!]. Without any doubt, the gymnastic fireman's red and black belt was the essential detail that defined being in court dress.

When I thought of this red and black belt I wondered if Sergeant Prosper hadn't bloodied his dark blue tunic running, elbows next to his sides, to Billancourt where duty called him, if not as certified rescuer, at least as a reenlisted noncommissioned officer and hard-as-nails survivor of Madagascar. But I wasn't very sure of it. Point-du-Jour, Issy-les-Moulineaux, and Billancourt were such special places, and everything associated with fire engines and firemen happened so much at the edge of the normal world!

Perhaps it was simply the concierge, dressed in court dress and no longer as a bank messenger, who started this race? Perhaps it was not Uncle Prosper but a completely different relative, or someone who happened to be visiting our apartment, which one reached by climbing three stories after crossing a vestibule and a courtyard? Perhaps it was young Poisson, the oldest son of the concierge, a boy who had come home one evening with his eye swollen and bloody because he had fallen getting off the tram? Perhaps it was only the firemen? And of course, in the end I knew that it was only they, when the ambiguity that had so delighted me was cleared up, and I realized that no one needed to put on court dress because we were only talking about Billancourt.

We learned a little later that the fire had been in the Ripolin factories. In the Paris metro stations in those days were large posters in glowing colors showing three painters in white blouses and straw hats, almost life-size. Each one held a can of Ripolin paint; they were standing in a single file, their backs slightly bent, and writing with their paintbrushes, the first on a wall, each of the other two on the back of the one in front of him, a few lines about the high quality of Ripolin paint.

Afterward, what I always thought when I stood on my lofty iron platform looking in the approximate direction of Point-du-Jour at the luminous sign of the Zigzag cigarette papers was how the innumerable cans of Ripolin paint stored in the factories must have burst into flame.

Point-du-Jour, *paranroizeuses,* Billancourt: barriers, borders, or limits, openworks of curving iron or scallops of arcades and houses. Through this latticework, I would glimpse something flickering, zigzags of lightning inscribed on a screen that was neither night nor day.[1]

In a way, Leiris's experiences are very new; however, we could also say that they belong to a very ancient dynasty, one that has been part of our literature since the Renaissance. And concerning those obscure monarchs, I think we could speak of the mystics of language, people who believed in the absolute, primal, and creative power of language, and language in its most material form: words, syllables, letters, even sounds.

It is here, in the carnal body of speech, that those strange philosophers, those aberrant poets found the beating heart of all meaning, the natural and divine storehouse of everything that can be said. For them, letters, sounds, words, like great sovereign shepherds, keep watch, alongside their primeval statures, over the flock of all future words. And in the eighteenth century there were a number of such credulous and poetic alphabets.

Here is an example:

At the sight of the Most High when Adam first spoke,
It was apparently the A that he uncloaked.

Soon stammered by the bumbling Bambino,
The B seemed to bound from his blundering beak;
He first learned to say bonsoir and bonjour;
Bonbons and bussing were bespoken in turn. [...]

The C rivals S when it has a cédille,
But without, it blocks Q, and in all our words teems,
Of all objects cuplike it commences the name;
Of a cave, a container, a chamber, a canon,
A crock or a core, a coffer or career, [...]

In deciding its tone though the D doesn't dally,
The tongue on the teeth it must rally;
And directly, tis its due, in discourse deploying
Its dorsal so arched, describes countless detours.

E strains with effort, exuded by breath,
Each time we respire, it escapes without stress;
And so in our tongue, by good fortune blessed,
In a word, even single, it is rarely repressed.
But so what if it flows in syllables complete;
A hidden interpreter of consonants silent,
Should one, by itself, ever dare to stray,
Behind or before it, we can then hear it bray. [...]

F in its fury, flutters and flaps, furrows, fights; [...]
Gives iron its force, it frisks and it fractures;
Gives birth to fire, flame, and fume,
And fecund in frost, in cold it is formed;
For a fabric we fold, it provides the effect,
And the fluttering frond and the flail when unchecked.

G, so much gayer, with R at its heels,
Approves with goodwill the grouping of graces;
A gasp of the voice will engender the G;
Which quivers at times in the gorge so engaged,
And at times from the I takes over its place,
Jousts in its place, it jazzes and japes,
But its general tone, which governs the globe,
Is much less chagrined when good taste is enthroned.

H, at the mouth's roof, has a hazardous birth,
Halts as it hastens the words it commands;

It hits and it harps, it inhales and hates,
And at times, out of honor, faint-hearted, it waits.

I, straight as a pike, assembles its empire,
Installed by the N by way of induction;
When I is impatient, laughter's betrayed,
And when it's protracted, ill fortune's delayed.

K long ago led the Kalends of Greece,
But left Q and C thus mortgaged in place;
And having come home, broken with age,
At Kimper alone does it find it's assuaged.

But L by itself how it gilds our language!
How lazily it flows, how lightly it floats;
The liquid of waves through it expressed,
Helps polish our style once it's been dressed;
Vowels are tinted, lashed with its color,
A bell peal for words? It's an oil that glows,
Deliquesces our phrases, and its lenitive sound
Consonants undoes, their rebellion unwound.

M in its turn on three legs makes its way,
And N by its side, on two legs does sway;
M moos in amusement, finds demise by immurement,
At the end of my nose, N runs off and resounds;
M loves to murmur, N in denial abounds;
N is for lampoons, M often mutinous;
Embedded in words, M marches with majesty,
N to nobility unites all necessity.

Our mouth goes around when O is in bloom,
And by force, we deploy an organ that booms,
When wonder, conceived in the brain up above,
Is wont to escape by this accent so novel.
The circle imparts a form so original,
It serves as an orbit as well as an oval;
We can't do without it when we must open,
And its order once given, it must be obeyed.[2]

In truth, I believe that the greatest of those mystics of language did not belong to the eighteenth century; he's much closer to us in time. He was an upstanding professor of French grammar, who lived during the late nineteenth century. His name is Jean-Pierre Brisset.[3] At the time, he was considered to be quite mad; André Breton knew of him.

Over the course of four books, he developed a prodigiously delirious etymology that ran the gamut from the croaking of frogs, our ancestors, to the most troubling, the most disturbing, and, in a sense as well, the most natural echoes of our present language. Shaking words like an obstinate rattle, repeating them in all sorts of ways, tearing from them derisive but also decisive harmonies, he brought fables into existence, through a kind of monstrous expansion, fables in which the entire history of mankind and the gods is contained, as if the world since its creation was nothing more than a gigantic word game, a glass-bead game that obeyed the most gratuitous, but also the most insuperable, laws:

> The comparison of languages unleashes the clarity and science of God, which shines in each language like the sun when it glows in its strength.
>
> Speech *[Parole]*, what are you? I am Pi, the power, Ar, which moves backward, Ol, which marches forward. I am perpetual motion in every direction, I am the image of suns and spheres and stars moving in a great expanse. Moving backward while marching forward. It is I, the queen and mother of mankind, who inhabits the globes. It is through me that the universe knows the universe.
>
> For seven years we have been in ecstasy before the marvels of speech; as long as the frog was only a frog, its language was unable to make much progress, but once the sexes began to make their presence known, strange, imperious sensations forced the animal to call out for assistance, for help, for it was unable to satisfy itself nor dampen the fires that consumed

it. The reason for this is that the frog's arms are short and its neck is held tightly by its shoulders. The development of the neck arrived at the same time and after the arrival of the sex that was the sign that one had been born. It was then said, he is born, neck is made when the neck was formed and it was a great joy to be born with hair, for the arrival of the neck gave rise to the stiff necks, from which we continue to suffer.

The anteriority of the syllable "mor" being well established, we find that it is, in effect, appropriate to the analysis of moralizing to lead toward mortality. Morbid, the color of mortality. Morsel, part of a whole that is dead *[mort]* or destroyed. Morseled, to divide that which is dead *[mort]* or destroyed. Mordant, which can result in mortality. To mope, to go around as if dead *[mort]*. To arm, to prepare for mortality.

Speech, tell us the future, what is eternity? It is the being who has departed, it is death, silence, it is everything that has lived. It is eternal and sullen remorse. What is the eternal? The eternal is nonbeing. The eternal is no more a being than the paternal is a father. But the supreme being is the god who is within us, who speaks and blossoms in his kingdom.

So many writers *[écrivains]*
So many vain-writings *[écrits-vains]*[4]

We know the importance in contemporary literature of these internal marvels of language. They are, I believe, the result of a paradox. This paradox is as follows: in one sense, all words are absolutely arbitrary, there is no natural need for us to call the sun the "sun" or the coolness of the earth "grass"; and yet language resonates within us, in our hearts and our memories, as something so old, so connected to all the things of the world, so close to their secret, that we have the impression of being able to discover all the horror of poetry by simply listening to them.

This has led to two myths that haunt contemporary literature, two complementary myths. First, there is the myth of a broken contract whereby words that have been agreed upon and accepted are replaced by others, but in such a way that the meaning would be conveyed all the same, just as limpid and obvious as if we were using the traditional words.

This is the ironic dream of a completely fiduciary language. For example, in this text by Tardieu, aren't we able to comprehend everything in his imagined dialogue? None of the appropriate words are employed but yet we find, brilliantly rendered, all of the most banal conventions of an exchange in a drawing room:

MADAME: Dear, dear fluffy! But how many holes has it been, how many pebbles has it been since I've had the baker's boy sugar you!

MADAME DE PERLEMINOUZE, *deeply touched*: Alas! My dear! I myself have been terribly vitreous! My three youngest crabs had lemonade, one after the other. For the entire beginning of the corsair, I did nothing but nestle windmills, run to the toy divers or the stool, I spent founts monitoring their carbide and giving them pliers and monsoons. To make a long story short, I didn't have a minuet to myself.

MADAME: Poor dear! And me, who didn't scratch at all!

MADAME DE PERLEMINOUZE: All the better! I'm so cooked! You certainly deserved to butter yourself after all the erasers you burned! Keep going, then. Why, from the Bullfrog's sulk to mid-Brioche, we didn't see you at the "Waterproof" or beneath the alpacas of the Migraine woods! You must have been gargled indeed!

MADAME, *sighing*: It's true! . . . Oh! What white lead! I can't even drop anchor there without a climb.

MADAME DE PERLEMINOUZE, *confidentially*: So, still no pralines?

MADAME: None.

MADAME DE PERLEMINOUZE: Not even a bit of parasol?

MADAME: Not a one! He never bothered to retouch me, ever since the flood when he striped me.

MADAME DE PERLEMINOUZE: What a snorer! But you should have raked his sparks!

MADAME: That's what I did. I scraped up four of them, five, maybe six in several pouts: but he never came clean.

MADAME DE PERLEMINOUZE: My dear little tisane! . . . *(Dreamy and alluring.)* If I were you, I would take another Chinese lantern.

MADAME: Impossible! It's obvious you don't slide at all! He has a terrible scarf over me. I'm his fly, his mitten, his duck; he's my rattan, my whistle; without him I can neither pinch nor screech; I'll never belt him in! *(Changing her tone.)* But, I'm tossing, will you float something, a blister of Zulu, two fingers of lotto?

MADAME DE PERLEMINOUZE, *accepting*: Thank you, with great daylight.

MADAME: *she rings, rings again in vain. Stands and calls*: Irma! . . . Irma, what are you doing! . . . Oh, that doe! She's as bent as a tree trunk . . . Excuse me, I have to go to the bar and mask that mule. I'll mend in a minuet.[5]

In contrast to this comic and derisive myth, we have the serious myth of a language that, on the contrary, would remain inside its own words. Because in the depths of its cave, it would find all the space needed for its creation. In a way, this language would need only to repeat itself, to dig its own soil, to expose unforeseen and yet necessary galleries of communication; and at that point all traces of convention would be erased and profound truths about nature and poetry would be exposed.

For example, isn't the wordplay whose alphabetical lexicon Michel Leiris employed in *Bagatelles végétales* the result of an obvious poetic necessity?

Adage of Jade:
>   Learn to gamble for pure appearance.
>   Idea, edi, edify, deify.
>   The manna of manes tumbles from tombs.
>   The hearth is a being, chairs are things.
>   Blood is the trail of time. Intoxication is the dream
>   and the chaff of viscera.
>   Deny nothing. Divine destiny.
>   Think of time, of tunnels, of your impotence, puppet.

[...]

Soul,
>   amical malice,
>   immaculately foamed lake.

Anguishing silken gloves ...

[...]

After the wind, after the flight, by sunrise.

Bitter arms. Arterial artilleries, torn by scarlet.

[...]

Lazy asylums of wings. Alliaceous trade winds.

[...]

On the rare dais of royalty, gilt with dawn.

April will release its tendrils. Foolish little fronds, jubilant
>   skies.

>   Brilliant with liberty ...

Vegetal bagatelles? Syllabic bacilli, ridiculous
>   rootlets.

[...]

Cadavers: frames and canvases wholesale, crusty carcasses,
>   cortege and cartilage spells.

Torrential centaurs, an angel glides along the widowed river.

Circle of rattles and gay glaives of wasps.

[...]

Hollow hearts, frigid frosts.

Drunken copulations beneath the cupola.

[...]

Poem: rebellious problem. Grass and wings (wings of feathers
    and skin, wrapped in their flight).
Present and piercing, how love labors you!
[...]
Vinous veins, avenues of venom: Venice?
Come, venerated and venereal nests, near our
        venomous knots!
[...]
Vertiginous, reveried refuge? Vampire or stryga,
        vaporous vertiges, appearances with rancid steps ...
Life drunk on the void. Lived and vesseled, from clamor to
        cavern.
[...]
Tufted vaults, boisterous boughs, base branches,
    new nerves for vision.[6]

So you see, there is nothing more marvelously lucid than this
patient attention to language shown by Leiris and Tardieu. And
yet, the perpetual play of language that the dream of these men
manifests and conceals, and the paralysis of hysterics as well,
or the rites of obsessives, or even the verbal labyrinth in which
schizophrenics lose their way—all of this probably does not have
a structure very different from the literary experiences we have
just seen; which does not mean that the language of madness
always has a literary signification, nor does it mean that literature today is fascinated or haunted by madness as it was at one
time by rebellion or passion or love. However, all this does imply
something important, which is that our age has discovered—and
almost simultaneously—that literature was at bottom merely a
fact of language and that madness was a signifying phenomenon. That both of them, as a result, played with signs, played
with *those* signs that play with us.

Literature and madness today have a common horizon, a kind
of common trunk, which is that of signs.

This break is probably like those horizon lines we can't escape from but that, nonetheless, can never be reached. Madness and literature may be, for us, like the sky and the earth joined all around us, but connected to one another by a kind of large opening in which we continue to advance, in which, in fact, we speak, we speak until the day they place a handful of dirt in our mouth.

I think that this, or something close to it, is what Artaud wanted to say in a text whose brilliance supremely conceals the path on which we, the rest of us, are forever getting lost:

> Yes, this is the only use language can now serve. A vehicle for madness, for the elimination of thought, for rupture, the maze of unreason.[7]

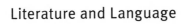

Literature and Language

In December 1964, Michel Foucault gave a lecture at the Facultés universitaires Saint-Louis in Brussels titled "Literature and Language." In promoting an analysis of the strange "triangulation" he identified between language, the literary work, and literature, Foucault reexamined the themes that could be found in his writing on literature in the early 1960s. During the first part of the lecture, whose tone appears to have been heavily influenced by references to Georges Bataille and Maurice Blanchot, the modern experience of literature (whose birth is historically situated by Foucault in a period ranging from the end of the eighteenth to the early nineteenth century) is described as the oscillation of language with itself, of which the literary work would be both the crystallization and the transgression. Foucault refers to authors that appeared frequently in his work throughout the 1960s (Sade, Cervantes, Joyce) along with others who were less commonly associated with his research (Proust, Chateaubriand, Racine, and Corneille). The second part of the lecture, which opens with an in-depth discussion of the work of the linguist Roman Jakobson, further explores the theme of a "structural esotericism" capable of affecting the way language is encoded. This encoding was exposed to its own recomposition: a gesture, eminently historical and linguistic, that involved the study of the restructuring of language at a given time and place (Foucault is already acting here, in his own way, as an archaeologist) and a far riskier engagement, conducted at the very frontier of existing linguistic determinations, with the disorder—or other order—within which the modern experience of literature would locate its primal moment.

What Is Literature?

IIIIIIIIIIIIIIIIIIIIIIIIIIIIIIIIIIIIIIIIIIIIIIIIIIIIIIIIIIIIIIIIIIIIIIIIIIIIIIIIIIIIIIIIIIIIIIIIIIIIIIIIIIIIIIIIIIIIIIIIIIIIIIIIIIIIIIIIII

As you know, the now famous question "What is literature?" is, for us, associated with the very practice of literature; as if the question hadn't been raised, after the fact, by a third party wondering about some strange object that lay outside itself, but had its place of origin precisely *within* literature, so that asking the question "What is literature?" became indistinguishable from the act of writing itself.

"What is literature?" is not at all the question of a critic, or a historian or sociologist, wondering about a particular fact of language. It's almost as if a cavity had been opened up within literature, a cavity in which the question resides and can gather together its entire being.

Yet, there is a paradox, in any case a difficulty. I've stated that literature is embedded in the question "What is literature?" But, after all, this question is quite recent; it is hardly older than we are. So, concerning the question "What is literature?" we can say that it was with the work of Mallarmé that it has come into view and has been formulated. But literature itself is timeless, it no more has a chronology or a civil status than human language itself.

However, I'm not sure that literature itself is as old as we often claim it to be. Of course, for millennia something has existed that, retrospectively, we are accustomed to call "literature."

But this is precisely what I believe we must call into question. It is far from certain that what Dante or Cervantes or Euripides did was literature. Of course, they belong to literature, which means that they are currently part of our literature, and that is because of a certain relationship that, in fact, only concerns us. They are part of our literature, they are not part of their own, for the excellent reason that Greek literature doesn't exist, Latin literature doesn't exist. In other words, if the relationship of Euripides's work to our language is indeed literature, the relationship of that same work to the Greek language was certainly not literature. To clarify, I would like to clearly distinguish three things.

First, there is language. As you know, language is the murmur of everything that is pronounced and, at the same time, it is this transparent system that results in the fact that when we speak, we are understood; in short, language is, at the same time, entirely the result of words accumulated throughout history as well as the system of language itself.

So, on one side we have language. On the other, we have literary works; let's just say there's this strange thing inside language, this configuration of language that dwells on itself, that remains motionless, that constitutes a space of its own, and which holds in that space the flow of the murmur, which thickens the transparency of signs and words, and which thus establishes a certain opaque volume, probably enigmatic, and that's what constitutes a literary work.

And there is also a third term, which is not exactly the literary work or language; this third term is literature.

Literature is not the general form of every work of language, nor is it the universal site where the work of language is situated. In a way it's a third term, the apex of a triangle through which passes the relationship of language to the work and the work to language.

I believe that it is a relationship of this sort that the word *literature* refers to as it is commonly accepted; "literature" in the seventeenth century would simply refer to the familiarity someone might have with works of language, usage, the frequency with which he reclaimed in his everyday language what was inherently a work. This relationship, which constituted literature in the classical age, was simply a matter of memory, of familiarity, of knowledge, a matter of reception.

But this relationship between language and the work, this relationship that traverses literature, at a certain moment ceased to be a purely passive relationship of knowledge and memory; it became an active relationship, practical, and consequently a relationship both profound and obscure between the work [at the moment of its creation and language itself; or between language at the moment of its transformation and the work it is in the process of becoming].[1] This moment when literature becomes the third, active term in the triangle thus formed, this moment is obviously the early nineteenth or the late eighteenth century, when, in the proximity of Chateaubriand, Madame de Staël, or de la Harpe,[2] the eighteenth century turned away from us, turned in upon itself, and carried with it something we no longer possess but which is worth thinking about if we intend to determine what literature is.

We are accustomed to saying that the critical conscience, the reflective uncertainty about the nature of literature appeared fairly late and, in a way, was accompanied by the rarefaction, the sullying of the literary work. This was at a time when, for purely historical reasons, literature was no longer capable of giving itself any object other than itself. In truth, it seems that the relationship of literature to itself, the question of what it is, was a part of its birth triangulation from the very beginning. Literature is not required for a language to transform itself into a work, nor does a work need to be fabricated with language; literature is a third point, different from language and different from the work, a third point that is external to their movement and, precisely for that reason, describes an empty space, an essential blankness in which the question "What is literature?" is born, an essential blankness that is this very question. As a result, this question cannot be superimposed upon literature, it is not added by a critical conscience that supplements literature, it is the very being of literature, originally dismembered and fractured.

It is not my intention to speak about anything in particular, not about the work, not about literature, not about language. But I would like to position my language, which unfortunately is neither a work of art nor literature, I would like to position it in that distance, in that divergence, in that triangle, in that dispersion of origin where the work, literature, and language dazzle one another, and by that I mean mutually illuminate and blind one another, so that perhaps, because of this, some aspect of their being will surreptitiously reach us. Maybe you'll be somewhat shocked and disappointed by the paucity of what I have to say.

But I would like very much that you pay attention to this paucity, because I want you to become aware of this cavity of language that has continued to dig into literature since its existence, which is to say, since the nineteenth century. I would like you to become cognizant of at least the need to jettison a platitude, an idea that literature specifically has constructed about itself, and this idea is as follows: literature is a language, a text made of words, of words like any others, but words that are so appropriately and carefully chosen and arranged that something ineffable passes through them.

It seems to me that just the opposite is the case. Literature is not at all made of something ineffable, it is made of something non-ineffable, of something we might consequently refer to, in the strict and original meaning of the term, as "fable." So, therefore, it is made from a fable, from something that must be said and that can be said, but this fable is said in a language that is absence, that is murder, that is doubling, that is simulacrum, because of which, it seems to me that a discourse on literature is possible, a discourse that would be something other than those allusions that have battered our ears now for hundreds of years, those allusions to silence, to secrecy, to the unsayable, to the

heart's modulations, and finally to all the attractions of individuality, where criticism, until recently, had sheltered its fickleness.

The first finding is that literature is not this brute fact of language that little by little allows itself to be penetrated by the
subtle, secondary question of its essence and its right to exist.
In itself, literature is a distance hollowed out within language, a
distance that is continuously traversed but never really crossed;
it is a kind of language that oscillates around itself, a kind of
standing vibration. But oscillation and vibration are inadequate
and not entirely appropriate because they lead us to assume
that there are two poles, that literature is at the same time part
of literature and equally part of language, and that there would
be something like hesitation between literature and language.
In fact, the relation to literature is understood entirely within the
absolutely immobile, motionless thickness of the work and, at
the same time, this relation is one by which the work and literature slip into each other.

When is the work, in a sense, literature? The paradox of the
work is precisely the fact that it is only literature at the very
moment of its beginning, [with its first sentence, with the blank
page. No doubt, it is truly literature only at that moment and on
that surface, in the preliminary ritual that provides words with
their space of consecration].[3] Consequently, once this blank
page begins to be filled up, once the words begin to be transcribed onto this still virgin surface, at that moment, every word
is in some sense absolutely disappointing in terms of literature,
for there is no word that belongs essentially, by some natural
right, to literature. In fact, once a word is written on the blank
page, which must be the page of literature, from that moment
on it is already no longer literature, that is, every real word is in
a way a transgression, which transgresses with respect to the
pure, white, empty, sacred essence of literature, which makes
every work not the fulfillment of literature but its rupture, its fall,
its violation. Every word without status or literary prestige is a

violation, every prosaic or ordinary word is a violation, but every word as soon as it's written is also a violation.

"For a long time, I went to bed early." This is how *In Search of Lost Time* begins. In a sense, it is indeed an entry into literature, but it is obvious that not one of these words belongs to literature; it's an entry into literature not because this sentence would be the entrance of a language fully armed with the signs, blazon, and marks of literature, but quite simply because it is the eruption of a language on an entirely blank page, the eruption of language without signs or arms, at the very threshold of something we'll never see in the flesh, words that lead us to the threshold of a perpetual absence that will become literature.

Moreover, it is characteristic that literature, ever since it has existed, since the nineteenth century, ever since it offered Western culture this strange figure we wonder about, it is characteristic that literature has always assigned itself a certain task, and that task is precisely the assassination of literature. Since the nineteenth century, it has no longer been a question, among the succession of literary works, of that contested, reversible relation—itself quite intriguing—which is the relation of old to new, which became the focus of self-examination for all of classical literature. The relation of succession, which appeared in the nineteenth century, is in a way a much earlier relation, one that is both the relation of literature's conclusion and literature's initial murder. Baudelaire is not to romanticism, Mallarmé is not to Baudelaire, surrealism is not to Mallarmé what Racine was to Corneille or Beaumarchais to Marivaux.

In reality, the historicity that appeared in the nineteenth century in the field of literature is a historicity of a quite special kind, one that, in any case, cannot be assimilated to the historicity that ensured the continuity or discontinuity of literature up to the eighteenth century. The historicity of literature in the nineteenth century does not entail the rejection of other works, or their disappearance, or their acceptance; the historicity of literature in the nineteenth century necessarily entails the rejection of literature itself, and this rejection of literature must be evaluated in terms of the very complex skein of its negations. Every new literary act, whether that of Baudelaire, or Mallarmé, or the surrealists, no matter who, implies at least four negations, four rejections, four attempted assassinations: first, the rejection of the literature of others; second, the rejection of the right of others even to make literature, to challenge the fact that the works of others might be literature; third, to deny oneself, to challenge one's right to make literature; and fourth, to refuse to do or say anything when using literary language other than the systematic, thoroughgoing murder of literature.

So, we can say that from the nineteenth century on, every literary act presented itself and was aware of itself as a transgression of that pure and inaccessible essence that literature was said to be. And yet, in another sense, every word, from the moment it's written on that famous blank page we wonder about, every word makes a sign. It makes a sign to something, for it is not like a normal word, an ordinary word. It makes a sign to something that is literature; every word, as soon as it's written on the blank page of the work, is a kind of indicator that blinks at something we call literature. For in truth, nothing in a work of language resembles what is said on a day-to-day basis. Nothing is part of real language, and I challenge you to find a single passage in any literary work that we could claim was really borrowed from the reality of everyday language.

And yet I realize that this does sometimes happen, I realize that some people have taken actual dialogues, some of them even recorded on tape, the way [Michel] Butor has done for his description of San Marco, where, to the description of the cathedral, he added tape-recorded passages reproducing the dialogue of several visitors, who commented, some about the cathedral itself and others about the quality of the ice cream sold nearby.

But the existence of real language thus excerpted and introduced into the literary work, when it occurs, is nothing more than a piece of paper stuck onto a cubist painting. The piece of paper is not there to make the painting "true"; on the contrary, it's there to break the space of the painting, and in the same way, true language, when it is actually introduced into a literary work, is put there to puncture the space of language, to give it a kind of sagittal dimension that, in fact, does not naturally belong to it. So that the work finally exists only to the extent that, at every moment, all the words are turned toward this literature, are illuminated by literature, and, at the same time, the work exists only because this literature is conjured and profaned, this literature that, nevertheless, supports each of those words, beginning with the very first.

So we can say that, all in all, the work as eruption disappears and is dissolved in this murmur that is the repetitiveness of literature; there is no work that doesn't thereby become a fragment of literature, a fragment that exists only because there exists around it, in front and back of it, something like the continuity of literature.

It seems to me that these two aspects, profanation and then this perpetually renewed sign of every word toward literature, it seems to me that this might enable us to outline two exemplary and paradigmatic figures of literature, two figures that are estranged and yet belong to each other.

One would be the figure of transgression, the figure of transgressive speech, and the other would be the figure of all those words that point to and signal to literature; so, on one side we have transgressive speech and, on the other, what I would call the repetitiveness of the library. One is the figure of the forbidden, of language at the limit, the figure of the jailed writer; the other is the space of books that continue to accumulate, that are stacked against one another, each of which has only a crenellated existence that delineates it and infinitely repeats it against the sky of all possible books.

It is obvious that Sade, at the end of the eighteenth century, articulated the first, the language of transgression. We can even say that his work is the point that simultaneously gathers and makes possible all transgressive speech. Sade's work, without a doubt, is the historical threshold of literature. In a sense, Sade's work is a gigantic pastiche. There isn't a single sentence in Sade that isn't entirely turned toward something that has been said before him by the philosophers of the eighteenth century, by Rousseau; there isn't a single episode, not a single one of those unbearable scenes that Sade narrates that isn't in reality the derisive, completely sacrilegious, pastiche of a scene in an eighteenth-century novel. We have merely to trace the names of the characters to discover those whom Sade wanted to profane.

This is to say that Sade's work claims to, claimed to wipe away all the philosophy, all the literature, all the language that came before it, and all that literature would be wiped away because transgressed by a language that would profane the page that had once more become blank. As for the unrestricted naming, as for the movements that meticulously run through all possibilities in Sade's famous erotic scenes, this is nothing other than a work reduced to the language of transgression alone, a work that, in a sense, erases every word ever written and by doing so exposes an empty space in which modern literature will take place. I believe that Sade is the very paradigm of literature.

And the figure of Sade, which is that of transgressive speech, has its double in the figure of the book, the book maintained in its eternity; it has its double, its opposite, in the library, which is to say, in the horizontal existence of literature, an existence that, in truth, is not simple, not univocal, but whose twin paradigm I believe would be Chateaubriand.

There is absolutely no doubt that the contemporaneity of Sade and Chateaubriand is not an accident of literature. From the outset, Chateaubriand's work, from its first line, seeks to be a book, it seeks to maintain itself at the level of the continuous murmur of literature, to transpose itself at once into this form of dusty eternity, which is that of the absolute library. It immediately seeks to rejoin the solid being of literature, thereby causing everything that might have been said or written before Chateaubriand to withdraw into a kind of prehistory. Therefore, we can say, to within a few years, that Chateaubriand and Sade constitute the two thresholds of contemporary literature. *Atala, or the Love of Two Savages in the Desert* and *La Nouvelle Justine, ou les Malheurs de la vertu* came into existence at approximately the same time. Naturally, it would be easy to compare or contrast these books. But what we should try to understand is the very system of their affiliation, this is the fold in which the modern experience of literature is born, at this moment, from the late eighteenth to the early nineteenth century, in such works, in such existences. This experience cannot be dissociated from transgression and death, it cannot be dissociated from the transgression Sade engaged in all his life, for which, as you know, he paid the price of liberty. As for death, you also know that it haunted Chateaubriand from the moment he began writing; it was obvious to him that the words he wrote only had meaning to the extent that he was, in a sense, already dead, to the extent that those words hovered somewhere beyond his life and beyond his existence.

It seems to me that this transgression and this passage beyond death represent two of the major categories of contemporary literature. If you prefer, we could say that in literature, in this form of language that has existed since the nineteenth century, there are only two real subjects, two speaking subjects—Oedipus for transgression and Orpheus for death. And there are only two figures who are spoken of, two figures who, at the same time, in hushed tones and almost indirectly, are addressed—they are the figure of the violated Jocasta and the figure of Eurydice, who is lost and subsequently found. These two categories, therefore, transgression and death, or, if you prefer, the forbidden and the library, distribute what might be called the inherent space of literature. In any event, it is from this place that something like literature comes to us. It is important to understand that literature, the literary work, does not arise from a kind of blankness that exists before language, but precisely from the repetitiveness of the library, the already deadly impurity of the word, and it is from this moment that language really makes a sign to us and, at the same time, to literature.

But what does it mean to say that the work makes a sign to literature? It means that the work calls literature, that it offers its bond, that it imposes upon itself a certain number of marks that prove to itself and to others that it is indeed literature. These—real—signs through which every word, every phrase indicates that it belongs to literature is what current criticism, ever since Roland Barthes, has called writing.

This writing makes every work, in a way, a small representation, like a concrete model of literature. It contains the essence of literature but, at the same time, provides its visible, real image. In this sense, we can say that every work not only says what it says, what it narrates, its story, its fable, but also, it says what literature is. Only, it doesn't say it twice, once for the content and once for the rhetoric; it says it all at once. This unity is indicated, precisely, by the fact that by the end of the eighteenth century rhetoric had disappeared.

That rhetoric has disappeared means that, from the moment of its disappearance, literature itself will be responsible for defining the signs and strategies by which it is going to become, precisely that, literature. Therefore, we can say that the job of literature, as it has existed ever since the disappearance of rhetoric, will not be to narrate something, or to add manifest and visible signs that it is literature—the signs of rhetoric—no, it will be obligated to employ a unique language and, yet, a language that is doubled, because, while telling a story, while narrating something, at every instant it will have to show and make visible what literature is, what the language of literature is, because of the disappearance of rhetoric, which was once responsible for telling us what beautiful language should be.

So, we can say that literature is a language that is both unique and subject to the law of the double; what happens to literature is what happens to the double in Dostoevsky[4]—this distance already present in the fog and the evening, this other figure whom we continue to meet at every street corner and who also happens to encounter the solitary walker, the moment of recognition occurring, in a moment of panic, only when face-to-face with the double.

A similar mechanism is at play between the literary work and literature. The work continuously anticipates literature; literature becomes a kind of double that appears before the work; the work, never recognizing it, continues to cross its path, but, significantly, it never succumbs to the moment of panic we find in Dostoevsky.

In literature, we never find the absolute encounter between the real work and flesh-and-blood literature. The work never encounters its double when it is finally present, and, to that extent, the work is the distance, the distance between language and literature; it is this space of doubling, this mirror space that we could call the simulacrum.

It seems to me that literature, the very being of literature, if we question what it is, could only respond one way, which is that there is no being of literature; there is simply a simulacrum, a simulacrum that is the entire being of literature. And Proust's work would very clearly show how literature is a simulacrum. We know that *In Search of Lost Time* is the story of a movement that does not lead from Proust's life to Proust's work but runs from the moment when Proust's life—his real life, his social life—is suspended, interrupted, closes in on itself, and to the very extent that life closes in on itself, the work will be able to begin and open up its own space.

But this life of Proust's, this real life, is never narrated in the work. And, on the other hand, this work, for which he suspended his life, for which he decided to interrupt his social life, this work is never given either; Proust tells us precisely how he's going to arrive at that work, the work that was to begin with the last line of the book, but that work, in reality, is never presented in its own body.

So, in *In Search of Lost Time,* the word *lost* has at least three meanings. First, it means that the time of life now appears closed, distant, irrecoverable, lost. Second, the time of the work, for which, precisely, there is no time in which to complete it because, when the text actually written is completed, the work is not yet there, the time of the work, which was unable to complete itself and which was supposed to narrate the genesis of the work, has, in a way, been wasted in advance: not only by living but by the story Proust creates about how he's going to write his work. And third, there is time without any fixed domicile, a time that lacks a date or a chronology, that floats freely as if it were lost between the muffled language of everyday life and the scintillating language of the finally illuminated work; this is the time we find in Proust's work itself, which appears to us in fragments, which we see as it floats freely, without any real chronology—it is a lost time, a time that can only be found as fragmentary flecks of gold. So that the work, in Proust, the work itself is never present in literature, for Proust's real work is nothing other than the project of creating a work, the project of making literature, but the actual work is unceasingly held back at the threshold of literature. At the precise moment when real language, which relates this arrival of literature, is about to become silent so that the work might finally appear in its sovereign, inevitable voice, at that very moment, the real work is completed, time is terminated, so that we can say that, in a fourth sense, time is lost at the very moment it is found.

You can see that in a work like Proust's, we can't say that

there's a moment that is actually the work; we can't say that there's a single moment that is actually literature. In fact, all of Proust's real language, all the language that we now read and call his work, which we refer to as literature, if we ask ourselves what it is, not for us but in itself, we realize that it is neither a work nor literature but a kind of intermediate space, a virtual space like the one we can see but never touch in mirrors, and it is this simulacral space that gives Proust's work its true volume.

To this extent, we need to recognize that Proust's project, the literary act he carried out when he wrote his work, in actuality has no assignable being, can never be situated at a given point of either language or literature; in fact, we find only a simulacrum, the simulacrum of literature. And the apparent importance of time in Proust simply arises from the fact that Proustian time, which is dispersion and atrophy on one side, the return and identity of moments of happiness on the other, is simply the internal projection—thematic, dramatized, narrated, recited—of this essential distance between the work and literature, which constitutes the profound being of literary language.

Thus, if we had to characterize the nature of literature, we would find this negative figure of transgression and the forbidden, symbolized by Sade; this figure of repetition, this image of the man who descends into the tomb with a crucifix in hand, this man who has never written anything other than from "beyond-the-grave," and ultimately, we would find the figure of death, symbolized by Chateaubriand; and then we would find this figure of the simulacrum. All are figures, I wouldn't say negative, but without any positive aspect at all, in which the being of literature seems to me to be fundamentally dispersed and torn apart.

But, in defining literature, maybe we're missing something essential. In any event, there is something we have yet to discuss, which is, however, historically very important in determining the nature of this form of language that appeared in the nineteenth century. It's obvious that transgression is no longer adequate for fully defining literature, for there were many transgressive literatures before the nineteenth century. And it's equally obvious that the simulacrum is no longer adequate to define literature because, before Proust, there was something like the simulacrum—look at Cervantes, who wrote the simulacrum of a novel, or Diderot with *Jacques the Fatalist*. In all these texts we find that virtual space in which there is neither literature nor work, but where there is a perpetual exchange between the work and literature.

"If I were a novelist," says Jacques the Fatalist to his master, "what I'm telling you would be far more beautiful than the reality I'm narrating; if I wanted to embellish everything I'm telling you, you would find that, at that moment, it would be a fine piece of literature, but I can't do it, I'm not writing literature, I'm obligated to tell you how things are."[5] And it is in this simulacrum of literature, this simulacrum of the rejection of literature, that Diderot writes a novel that is, fundamentally, the simulacrum of a novel. In fact, this problem of the simulacrum, in Diderot, for example, and in literature after the nineteenth century, is important because it helps introduce us to what seems to me to be central to the fact of literature. In *Jacques the Fatalist,* you know that the story will unfold on several levels. First, there is the story by Diderot of the voyage and the six dialogues between Jacques, the so-called Fatalist, and his master. Then, this story by Diderot is interrupted by the fact that Jacques, in a way, takes over for Diderot and begins to narrate his love affairs. And then, the story of Jacques's love affairs is again interrupted, this time by a third-level narrative, by a series of third-level narratives in which the hostesses or the captain, for example, narrate their own stories. And, thus, we have, within the narrative, layers of narrative inside one another, like some Japanese doll,[6] and this is what constitutes the pastiche of the adventure novel that we know as *Jacques the Fatalist.*

But what is important, what seems to me entirely characteristic, is not only this nesting of stories inside one another, but the fact that at every moment, Diderot, in a way, causes the narrative to jump backward and imposes on these nested stories what might be called retrograde figures who constantly lead us toward a type of reality, the reality of a neutral language, of the first language, which would typify everyday language, the language of Diderot himself, the very language of his readers.

And these retrograde figures are of three kinds. First, we have the reactions of characters in the nested stories, who continuously interrupt the story they are being told. Second, there are the characters who appear in a nested story—at a given moment, the hostess narrates the story of someone we don't see, someone who is simply a virtual guest inside the story, and then, in Diderot's story, this real character suddenly appears, whereas in reality, his only status was to be nested within the story told by the hostess. Third, at every moment Diderot turns to his reader to tell him, "You must find what I'm telling you rather extraordinary but that's how it happened. Of course, this adventure doesn't conform to the rules of literature, it doesn't conform to the rules of well-written narratives, but I'm not in control of my characters, they overwhelm me, they've come into view along with their past, their adventures, their enigmas. I'm simply telling you what actually happened." Thus, from the most densely sheathed, the most indirect core of the narrative to a reality that is contemporary, even anterior to writing, in a way Diderot does nothing other than to detach himself from his own literature. He continuously shows us that this, all of this, is not literature and that there is an immediate, a first language, the only one that is solid and on which are constructed, arbitrarily and for the pleasure of it, the stories themselves.

This structure is characteristic of Diderot, but we also find it in Cervantes and in innumerable narratives from the sixteenth to the eighteenth century. For literature, that is to say, for the form of language that began in the nineteenth century, games like those found in *Jacques the Fatalist,* are in reality merely frivolous.

For example, when Joyce decides to write a novel that is, if you will, based entirely on *The Odyssey,* he doesn't do it at all like Diderot when he constructed a novel on the model of the picaresque novel. In fact, when Joyce repeats Ulysses, he does so in such a way that in this fold of language, repeated within itself, something appears that is not, as in Diderot, the language of the everyday but something that is like the birth of literature itself. That is, Joyce writes so that, within his story, within his sentences and the words he employs, within this infinite story of a day in the life of a man like any other in a city like any other, something occurs that is both the absence of literature and its imminence, which is the fact that literature is there, absolutely, and it is absolutely there because it's about Ulysses but, at the same time, in the distance, in some way as close as possible to his remoteness.

No doubt this leads to that configuration essential to Joyce's *Ulysses*: on the one hand, there are circular figures, the circle of time, which runs from morning till evening of the same day, and the circle of space, which surrounds the city in which the main character walks around. Then, outside these circular figures, you have a kind of perpendicular and virtual relationship, a point-by-point relationship, a one-to-one relationship between each episode of Joyce's *Ulysses* and each adventure in *The Odyssey.* And through this reference, at every moment, the adventures of Joyce's character are not doubled and superimposed, on the contrary, they are hollowed out by this absent presence of the character of *The Odyssey,* who is himself the possessor, but the absolutely distant and never accessible possessor of literature.

To summarize, we might say that the work of language in the classical age was not truly literature. Why is it that we can't say that *Jacques the Fatalist* or Cervantes, why can't we say that Racine is literature, or Corneille, or Euripides, except for us, of course, to the extent that we incorporate them into our language? Why is it that, at this very moment, Diderot's relationship to his own language was not the literary relationship I've just spoken about? It seems to me that we could say the following: in the classical age, in any event at the end of the eighteenth century, every work of language existed as a function of a certain silent and primitive language, which the work was responsible for restoring. This silent language was, in a way, the initial, the absolute source from which every work would subsequently break off, and within which it had lodged. This silent language, this language before languages, was the word of God, the truth, the template, it was the Ancients, it was the Bible, giving to the word *Bible* its absolute sense, that is to say, its common sense. There was a kind of preexisting book, which was truth, which was nature, which was the word of God, and which hid within him, and which at the same time stated the whole truth.

And this sovereign and restrained language was such that, on the one hand, every other language, every human language, when it wanted to become a work, simply had to retranslate, retranscribe, repeat, or restore it. But, in another sense, this language of God or this language of nature or this language of truth was hidden. It was the foundation of every revelation and yet was itself hidden, it could not be directly transcribed. From this arose the need for those shifts, those twisting words, the entire system we refer to as rhetoric. After all, what are metaphors, metonymy, synecdoche, and so on, if not the attempt to rediscover, using human words, which are obscure and hidden from themselves, through the interplay of openings and obstructions, to rediscover this silent language the work had as its meaning and whose task it was to reinstate and restore?

In other words, between a loquacious language that says nothing and an absolute language that says everything but reveals nothing, there had to be an intermediary language, one that led from loquacious language to the silent language of nature and God, namely, literary language. If we define signs, with Berkeley and the philosophers of the eighteenth century, as that which was spoken by nature or by God, we can say, quite simply, that the classical work is characterized by the fact that it involved, through the interplay of figures, which were the figures of rhetoric, converting the density, the opacity, the obscurity of language into the transparency, the very luminosity of signs.

On the contrary, literature began when, for the Western world, for a part of the Western world, this language, which had never stopped being heard, never stopped being perceived or assumed for millennia, became silent. Beginning in the nineteenth century, we stopped listening for this originary speech and in its place could be heard the infinite murmur, the accumulation of words already spoken. Under these conditions, the work no longer has to be embodied in the figures of rhetoric that would serve as signs of a silent, absolute language. The work no longer has to speak other than as a language that repeats what has been said and which, through the force of repetition, simultaneously erases everything that has been said and brings it closer to itself, to take hold of the essence of literature.

We could say that literature began the day something we might call the volume of the book was substituted for the space of rhetoric. And it's very strange to realize that it was only quite late that the book became an event in the being of literature. It took four centuries after it had been actually, technically, materially invented for the book to assume its status in literature. And Mallarmé's book is the first book of literature, Mallarmé's book, this fundamentally flawed project, one that could not but fail, is, one might say, the result of Gutenberg's success over literature. Mallarmé's book, which would repeat and, at the same time, destroy all other books, a book that, in its blankness, caresses the being that escaped literature once and for all, responds to this great silent book filled with signs that the classical work attempted to copy, to represent. Mallarmé's book responds to this great book but, at the same time, substitutes itself for it: it is the acknowledgment of its disappearance.

We can now see why, in its prestige, and not only in its prestige but in its essence, on the one hand, the classical work was nothing other than a re-presentation, for it had to re-present a language that was already established, which is why, at bottom, the very essence of the classical work can always be found in theater, whether in Shakespeare or Racine, for we're in the world of representation; and conversely, the essence of literature, in the strict sense of the term, from the nineteenth century on, is not found in the theater but, precisely, in the book.

And it is finally in this book, which of all other books is lethal and, at the same time, takes upon itself the always disappointing project of making literature, it is finally in this book that literature finds and founds its being. Although the book existed, and with a very dense reality, for several centuries prior to the invention of literature, it was not, in fact, the site of literature: it was merely a material opportunity for transmitting language. The best proof is that *Jacques the Fatalist* escaped, or ceaselessly sought to escape, the sorcery of adventure novels through the retrogression we've spoken about, as did Don Quixote and Cervantes.

But in fact if literature fulfills its being in the book, it doesn't placidly welcome the essence of the book (besides, the book, in reality, has no essence, has no essence other than what it contains); that is why literature will always be the simulacrum of the book, it behaves as if it were a book, it pretends to be a series of books. That is also why it can only be fulfilled through aggression and violence toward all other books; not only that, but aggression and violence directed against the plastic, derisive, feminine essence of the book. Literature is transgression, literature is the virility of language compared to the femininity of the book; but what can it be, ultimately, other than one book among all the others, one book with all the others, in the linear space of the library? What can literature be, precisely, other than the frail, posthumous existence of language? That's why it's not possible for this literature, now that its entire being is in the book, it's not possible, in the end, for it to be anything other than from beyond the grave.

Thus, what is gathered in this single thickness of the book, open and closed, in those leaves that are simultaneously blank and covered with signs, in this unique volume—for each book is unique and similar to all the others for all books resemble one another—is something like the very being of literature. This literature that should not be understood as the language of mankind, nor as the word of God, nor as the language of nature or the language of the heart or silence; literature is a transgressive language, it is a mortal, repetitive, redoubled language, the language of the book itself. There is only one speaking subject in literature, one alone, and it is the book, this thing that Cervantes, as you may recall, had so desperately wanted to burn, this thing that Diderot, in *Jacques the Fatalist,* had so often tried to escape, this thing in which Sade had been imprisoned and in which we, we too, are imprisoned.

What Is the Language of Literature?

llllllllllllllllllllllllllllllllllllllllllllllllllllllllllllllllllllllllllllllllllllllllllllllllllllllllllllllllllll

Yesterday, I presented, or tried to present, several thoughts about literature, about this antithetical and simulacral being embodied in the book. This evening, I'd like to take a step back and try to slightly circumvent the statements I made about literature. For, after all, is it really so clear, so obvious, so immediate that we can speak of literature? For, when we speak of literature, what do we have as our floor, as our horizon? No doubt, nothing more than the void surrounding literature, which results in something that is quite strange and possibly unique, namely, that literature is an infinite language that allows for endless discussion.

What is this perpetual reduplication of literature by language about literature? What is this language of literature, which gives rise to exegeses, commentaries, and redoublings ad infinitum? The problem, I feel, is not clear. It is not clear in itself and it seems to me that it is less clear than ever today.

There are several reasons for this. First, a change has occurred quite recently in what we might call criticism. We could say that the layer of critical language has never been thicker than it is today. Never has this second language, known as criticism, been used so frequently and, reciprocally, never has the absolutely first language, the language that speaks only of itself and in its own name, been proportionally thinner than it is today.

Yet, this thickness, this multiplication of critical acts, has been accompanied by an almost contrary phenomenon, which is as follows: the figure of the critic, *Homo criticus,* which was invented more or less in the nineteenth century between La Harpe and Sainte-Beuve, is in the process of being erased at the very moment when the number of critical acts has multiplied.[1] This is to say that critical acts, through their proliferation and dispersal, have spread and no longer lodge in texts devoted to criticism but in novels, poems, essays, and possibly philosophies. Today, true acts of criticism are found in the poems of René Char or in Maurice Blanchot's fragments, and in texts by Francis Ponge, much more so than in any given parcel of language that will have been explicitly, and because of the name of its author, intended as a critical act. We could say that criticism has become a general function of language in general but without an institution, without its own subject.

And yet—and this would be the third phenomenon that makes it difficult to understand contemporary literary criticism—yet, today, a new phenomenon has appeared, which is as follows: we have seen the establishment, from language to language, of a relationship that is not exactly one of criticism, in any case not one that is consistent with the traditional notion of criticism, this judgmental, hierarchizing institution, this mediating institution between a creative language, a creative author, and a public seen simply as consumers. Today, a very different relationship has been formed between what we might call the first language, and which we will simply call literature, and this second language, which speaks of literature and which we ordinarily call criticism. In effect, criticism is currently being made use of by two new types of relationship being established between itself and literature.

Criticism today seeks to establish, with respect to literature, with respect to the first language, a kind of objective network, one that is discursive, justifiable at each of its points, and demonstrable, a relationship in which what is most important, what is constitutive, is not the taste of the critic, a taste that is more or less secret, or more or less manifest, but a necessarily explicit method, a method of analysis—it could be psychoanalytic, linguistic, thematic, formal, what have you. Therefore, you could say that criticism is in the process of presenting the problem of its foundation within the order of positivity, or science.

Yet, on the other hand, criticism plays an entirely new role, which is nothing like the role it once had, which was as an intermediary between writing and literature. From the time of Sainte-Beuve until the present, what, after all, did it mean to do criticism? It meant engaging in a kind of first, privileged reading, a reading prior to all the others and which helped make the author's writing—necessarily somewhat opaque, obscure, or esoteric—accessible to readers of the second zone, which would include all of us, all of us readers who need criticism to understand what we're reading. In other words, criticism was the privileged, absolute, and first form of reading.

It seems to me now, however, that what's important in criticism is that it is in the process of going over to the side of writing. And this happens in two ways. First, because criticism is becoming increasingly interested not in the psychological moment of the creation of the work but in writing itself, in the very thickness of the writing of writers, a writing that has its own forms, its own configurations. And second, because criticism has stopped wanting to be a better or earlier or better prepared form of reading; criticism is in the process of itself becoming an act of writing. No doubt writing that is second with respect to another but, just the same, writing that forms, with all the other forms of writing, a maze, a network, an interlacing of points and lines. These points and lines of writing in general intersect, repeat, cover one another, shift places, to form, in the end, a total neutrality, which we could call the totality of criticism and literature—the actual floating hieroglyph of writing in general.

You can see the ambiguity we are faced with in trying to comprehend the nature of this second language, which has just been added to the first language of literature and which also claims to maintain, in relation to that first language, a discourse that is absolutely positive, explicit, completely discursive and demonstrable, and which, at the same time, tries to be an act of writing, like literature. How can we resolve this paradox? How can criticism be both this second language and, at the same time, function as a first language? That's what I'd like to try to clarify here, to determine what, after all, is criticism?

Quite recently, maybe ten years ago, no more than that, in attempting to explain the nature of criticism, a linguist by the name of Roman Jakobson introduced a concept he had borrowed from logicians, the concept of a metalanguage.[2] Jakobson suggested that criticism, like grammar, like stylistics, like linguistics in general, was a metalanguage. Obviously, this is a very seductive concept and appears, at least at first glance, to be perfectly applicable given that the concept of a metalanguage puts us in the presence of two properties that are, at bottom, essential for defining criticism. The first is the possibility of defining the properties of a given language, its forms, its codes, its laws, in another language. And the second property of a metalanguage is that this second language, in which we can define the forms, laws, and codes of the first language, this second language is not necessarily different in substance from the first language. Because, after all, we can use French as the metalanguage of French, or German, or English, or any language. We can also use a symbolic language invented for this purpose. Consequently, we have here, in this possibility of absolute distance from the first language, the possibility of utilizing a discourse that is entirely discursive and yet of being entirely on the same plane as that language.

I'm not sure, however, that this concept of a metalanguage, which appears to define, at least abstractly, the logical site where criticism might reside . . . it doesn't seem to me that this concept should be used to define criticism. To explain this reticence with respect to the concept of a metalanguage, we should perhaps return to what we were discussing yesterday about literature. You may recall that the book had appeared as the site of literature, that is, as the space in which the work becomes the simulacrum of literature, in an interplay of mirroring and unreality, where it was a question of both transgression and death. If we attempt to express the same thing using the vocabulary of language specialists, perhaps we could say something like the following: literature is, of course, one of the countless speech phenomena that are effectively uttered by mankind. Like all speech phenomena, literature is possible only to the extent that those words *[paroles]* are indistinguishable from language in general *[langue]*, from that general horizon that constitutes the code of a given language. Therefore, all literature, as a speech act, is possible only with respect to that language, only with respect to the structures and codes that make each word of the language an actual utterance, that make it transparent, that allow it to be understood. If sentences have a meaning, it is because each speech phenomenon is housed within the virtual but absolutely restrictive scope of the language. Of course, these ideas are now very well known.

But couldn't we say that literature is an extremely unique speech phenomenon, and probably distinct from all other speech phenomena? In effect, literature, at bottom, is speech that may obey the code in which it is placed but that, at the very moment of its inception, and in each of the words it utters, compromises the code in which it is situated and understood. This is to say that, whenever someone picks up a pen to write something, it's literature to the extent that the constraint of the code is suspended in the very act of writing the word—this suspension being such that, at some point, the word might very well not obey the code of the language. If every word written by a writer really did fail to obey the code of the language, there is absolutely no way it could be understood, and this would absolutely be the speech of madness—which may be the reason for the essential relationship between literature and madness today. But that's another question. We can simply state that literature is the risk always taken and always assumed by each word of a sentence of literature, the risk that, after all, this word, this sentence, and all the rest, might not obey the code. Take the two sentences, "For a long time, I went to bed early" and "For a long time, I went to bed early," the first being the one I speak, the second being the one I read in Proust. Those two sentences are verbally identical; in reality they are profoundly different. From the moment they were written by Proust at the beginning of *In Search of Lost Time,* it's possible that none of those words has had exactly the same meaning we give to them when we utter them in our daily lives; it's very possible that speech has suspended the code from which it has been borrowed.[3]

We could say that there is a risk, always essential, fundamental, always ineradicable in all of literature, the risk of structural esotericism. It's very possible that the code might not be respected; in any event, literary speech always has the sovereign right to suspend the code, and it's the presence of this sovereignty, even if it is not, in fact, exercised, that probably constitutes the uncertainty and the grandeur of every work of literature. To that extent, it does not seem to me that a metalanguage would really be applicable as a method of literary criticism, that it could be proposed as the logical horizon against which we might identify what criticism is. Because a metalanguage specifically implies that we have a theory that covers all speech actually uttered based on the code that has been established for the language. If the code is compromised in speech, if at some point the code ceases to have absolute value, at that moment, it's no longer possible to establish a metalanguage for such speech; we're forced to rely on other means. Where do we turn, then, in defining literature if we no longer turn to the concept of a metalanguage?

Perhaps we should be more modest and, rather than rashly advancing this hoary term from logic, that of a metalanguage, simply acknowledge a nearly imperceptible piece of evidence, but one I find to be decisive, namely, that language may be the only being in the world that is absolutely repeatable.

Of course, there are other beings in the world that are repeatable; there are two of the same animal, two of the same plant. But in the natural order, repetition is, in reality, only a partial identity and, moreover, one that can be easily analyzed discursively. There are no repetitions in the strict sense outside the order of language. And one day we will have to analyze all the possible forms of repetition in language, and it may be through the analysis of these forms of repetition that we'll be able to outline something like an ontology of language. For now, we can simply state that language never stops repeating itself.

Linguists are very familiar with this idea and have shown how only a small number of phonemes are needed to constitute the total vocabulary of a language. Those same linguists, as well as the authors of dictionaries, know how few words are needed, ultimately, to account for all possible utterances, an infinite number, a necessarily open quantity, and those are the utterances we pronounce every day. We continuously speak a certain repetitive structure—phonetic repetition, the semantic repetition of words; we also know that language can be repeated as it is spoken and at the moment of utterance: we can say the same sentence, we can say the same thing with other words, and it is precisely this that makes up exegesis, commentary, and so on. We can even repeat the form of a language, entirely suspending its meaning, and this is what language theorists do whenever they repeat a language through its grammatical or morphological structure.

In any event, you can see that language is in some way probably the only site of being in which something like repetition is absolutely possible. This phenomenon of repetition in language is, of course, a constitutive property of language, but this property is not neutral and inert with respect to the act of writing. Writing does not mean sidestepping the necessary repetition of language; I believe that writing, in the literary sense, involves placing repetition at the very heart of the work. And maybe we would have to say that literature—Western literature, of course, for I'm unfamiliar with the others and don't know what we could say about them—Western literature had to have begun with Homer, who made use of an astonishing repetitive structure in *The Odyssey*. Recall book 8 of *The Odyssey*, where we find Ulysses among the Phaeacians but not yet recognized by them. Ulysses is invited to a banquet by the Phaeacians but no one recognizes him. His strength in the games, his triumph over his adversaries, were the only things that showed he was a hero, but they did not betray his true identity. So he is both present and hidden. And in the midst of the banquet, a bard arrives: he's come to sing of the adventures of Ulysses, he's come to sing of the exploits of Ulysses, adventures and exploits that are being pursued before the eyes of the bard, because Ulysses is present. These exploits, which are far from being completed, thus contain their own narrative as one of the episodes because it is part of Ulysses's adventures that, at a given moment, he will hear a bard sing of the adventures of Ulysses. And in this way, *The Odyssey* is repeated within itself, it possesses a kind of central mirror, at the heart of its own language, so that Homer's text turns around itself, wraps around or unfurls around its center, and is repeated in a movement that is essential to it. It seems to me that this structure, which we find very often—we find it in *The Arabian Nights*, for example, where one of the nights is devoted to the story of Shahrazad narrating the thousand and one nights to a sultan to escape death—is probably constitutive of the very being of literature, if not in general, at least of Western literature.

It is likely, even certain, that there is a very important distinction between this repetitive structure and the internal repetitive structure we find in modern literature. In *The Odyssey*, we find the infinite song of the bard who, in a way, pursued Ulysses and tried to catch up with him; and at the same time, we have this song of the bard, who has always already begun and who has just met Ulysses, who welcomes him into his own legend and makes him speak at the very moment of his silence, reveals him as he hides himself. In modern literature, the self-referentiality is probably much more silent than this lengthy dislocation narrated by Homer. It's likely that it is in the thickness of its language that modern literature repeats itself and, most likely, through this interplay of speech and code, which I spoke of a moment ago.

I would like to conclude these thoughts on metalanguage and repetitive structures by saying, by suggesting the following: couldn't we, at this time, define criticism, very naively, not as a metalanguage but as the repetition of what is repeatable in language? And to that extent, literary criticism could probably be included in the great exegetical tradition that began, at least for the Greek world, with the first grammarians who produced commentaries on Homer. Couldn't we say, as a first approximation, that criticism is purely and simply the discourse of doubles, that is, the analysis of distances and differences in which the identities of the language are distributed? And at that moment, we would find that three forms of criticism are possible. The first would be the science, or knowledge, or repertory of figures by which identical elements of language are repeated, varied, combined—how we vary, combine, repeat phonetic elements, semantic elements, syntactic elements. Criticism, in this sense, as a science of the formal repetitions of language, has a name and has existed for a long time; it's known as rhetoric. There is a second form of the science of doubles, which would be the analysis of identities or modifications, or mutations of meaning through the diversity of languages—how it is that we can repeat a meaning using different words. And you know that this is pretty much what criticism has done in the classical sense of the term, from Sainte-Beuve until approximately today, when we try to rediscover the identity of a psychological or a historical meaning, that is, the identity of a given thematization, throughout the plurality of a work. This is what is traditionally called criticism.

I wonder if there might not be a place, or if a place doesn't already exist, for a third form of criticism, namely, the deciphering of this self-referentiality, this implication of the work in itself, in the thick structure of repetition, which I spoke about earlier in reference to Homer. Couldn't there be a place for the analysis of this curve by which the work always points to itself within itself and presents itself as the repetition of language by language? This seems to me to be more or less the case: the analysis of this implication of the work itself, the analysis of those signs through which the work continuously refers to itself within itself; I think it is this, in short, that provides meaning to the diverse and polymorphous endeavors currently referred to as literary analysis.

And I'd like to show how this concept of literary analysis, which is used and applied by very different people—Barthes, Starobinski,[4] and so on—how this literary analysis can serve as the basis for a consideration, that is, how it can expose and unlock a *quasi*-philosophical consideration—for I don't claim to do real philosophy any more than I claimed yesterday that literary professionals do real literature: I would be in the simulacrum of philosophy just as yesterday literature was in the simulacrum of literature. So, I would like to know if these literary analyses might not be leading us toward a simulacrum of philosophy.

It seems to me that the outlines of literary analysis that have been provided so far could be grouped together; in any case, we could assign two different directions to them. One involves the signs by which works refer to themselves within themselves; and the other concerns the way in which the distance that works assume within themselves is spatialized.

I'd first like to speak, purely programmatically, of the analyses that have been done, and which could be done, probably, to show how literary works continue to be internally self-referential. You know, it's a paradoxically recent discovery that the literary work is made not with ideas, not with beauty, especially not with feelings, but that the literary work is simply made with language. That is, it's based on a system of signs. But this system of signs is not isolated. It is part of an entire network of other signs, which are the signs that circulate in a given society, signs that are not linguistic, but signs that can be economic, monetary, religious, social, and so on. Every time we choose to study the history of a culture, there exists a certain sign state, a general state of signs in general, which means that we need to establish the elements that serve as supports for signifying values and the rules those signifying elements follow as they circulate.

To the extent that it is a deliberate manipulation of verbal signs, we can be certain that the literary work is part, regionally, of an ever flickering horizontal network—whether silent or verbose makes little difference—that, at every moment in the history of a culture, forms what we could refer to as a sign state. Consequently, to find out how literature signifies itself, we need to find out how it is signified, where it is situated in the world of signs of a given society, something that has practically never been done for contemporary societies, something that should be done, possibly by using as a model a work that concerns cultures much more archaic than our own. I'm thinking of the work done by Georges Dumézil on Indo-European societies.[5]

Dumézil showed how Irish legends, Scandinavian sagas, the historical tales of the Romans, as found in Titus-Livius, and Armenian legends, how all of them, which we could refer to as language works if we want to avoid the word *literature,* how all those works of language are, in reality, part of a much more general sign structure. And we can only understand what those legends really are if we reestablish the structural homogeneity that exists between them and, for example, a given religious or social ritual found in some other Indo-European society. In light of this, we see that, in such societies, literature functioned like an essentially social and religious sign, and it is to the extent that it assumed the signifying function of a religious or social ritual that literature existed, that it was both created and consumed.

Today, it is quite probable—it would have to be shown, we would have to establish the status of signs currently existing in our society—it is quite probable that literature would not be associated with religious signs but with the signs, let's say, of consumption or the economy. But at present, we don't know how those signs function, it's this first semiological layer, establishing the signifying region occupied by literature, that we would need to investigate.

Compared to this first semiological layer, we can say that literature is inert. Of course, it functions, but the network in which it functions does not belong to it, is not dominated by it. Consequently, we need to push this semiological analysis or, rather, develop it in the direction of another layer that would be internal to the work. This means we would have to establish the nature of the sign system that functions, not within this given culture, but within the work itself. Here too, we are still dealing with fundamentals in a way, with exceptions. Ferdinand de Saussure[6] left several notebooks in which he, in fact, attempted to define the use and structure of phonetic or semantic signs in the literature of the Romance languages. Those texts were published by Starobinski in the *Mercure de France.*[7] There he provides an outline of an analysis in which literature appeared essentially as a combination of verbal signs. There are some authors for whom such analyses are straightforward. I'm thinking of Charles Péguy, Raymond Roussel, of course, the surrealists as well, and there would be, in the analysis of the verbal sign as such, there would be, you could say, a possible second layer of semiological analysis, a layer that would no longer be that of cultural semiology but of linguistic semiology, which defines the choices that can be made, the structures to which those choices are subjected, why they were made, and the degree of latency that is given at each point of the system and which signifies the internal structure of the work. There is probably also a third layer of signs, a third network of signs that are used by literature to signify itself. This would involve the signs that Roland Barthes called the signs of writing. That is to say, the signs by which the act of writing is ritualized outside the domain of immediate communication.

We now know that writing is not simply the use of the formulas of an era while mixing in a few individual formulas; writing does not involve mixing a certain amount of talent, mediocrity, or genius, writing primarily implies the use of signs that are nothing other than signs of writing. Those signs may be words, certain so-called noble words, but they are mostly deep linguistic structures, such as verb tenses in French. Flaubert's writing, for example, consists essentially—and we can say the same of all the classical French narratives from Balzac to Proust—of a certain configuration, a certain relationship between the imperfect, the past historic, the perfect, and the pluperfect, a constellation that is never found with the same values in the language used by you and me, or in the newspaper. In French narrative, this configuration of four tenses is what establishes that it is, precisely, a literary narrative.

Finally, we need to add a fourth semiological layer, one that is much more limited and discrete. This would be the study of what we could call signs of implication, or self-implication. These are the signs with which a work refers to itself internally, re-presents itself in a certain form, with a certain face. Earlier, I spoke of book 8 of *The Odyssey,* in which Ulysses listens to the bard singing of the adventures of Ulysses. There is something highly characteristic about this scene. For, when he hears the bard singing about his own adventures, Ulysses, who has still not been recognized by the Phaeacians, lowers his head, covers his face, and begins to cry, as Homer's text describes, with a gesture characteristic of women when they receive the corpse of their spouse after a battle.

Here, the sign of the self-implication of literature is highly significant; it's a ritual, specifically, the ritual of mourning. Which is to say that the work refers to itself only in death, and only in the death of the hero. The work exists only to the extent that the hero, who is alive in the work, is nonetheless already dead in terms of the story that has been created.

If we compare this sign of self-implication to the sign of self-implication in the work of Proust, we find highly interesting and characteristic differences. The internal self-implication found in *In Search of Lost Time,* on the contrary, appears in the form of timeless illumination, when suddenly, in the presence of a damask napkin, or a madeleine, or the unevenness of the cobblestones in the Guermantes's courtyard, which recall the unevenness of the cobblestones in Venice, something like the timeless, illuminated, absolutely joyous presence of the work appears to the very person who is in the process of writing it. Between this timeless illumination and Ulysses's gesture of veiling his face and crying like a wife accepting the corpse of her husband killed in battle, you can see there is an absolute difference, and that a semiology of such signs of the internal self-implication of works would certainly tell us many things about the nature of literature. But such an attempt has almost never been carried out. If I've insisted on these different semiological layers it's because, currently, there's a certain confusion about the use of linguistic and semiological methods in literature. There are some today who use linguistic methods for everything and treat literature as a raw fact of language.

It's true that literature is made with language, the way architecture is made with stone. But we shouldn't conclude that it's possible to indifferently apply to it the structures, concepts, and laws that are valid for language in general. In fact, when we apply semiological methods directly to literature, we're victims of confusion twice over. On the one hand, we resort to the recurrent use of a particular signifying structure in the field of signs in general; that is, we forget that language, after all, is only one sign system among a much more general system of signs, namely, the religious, social, economic signs I spoke of earlier. And, on the other hand, by applying linguistic analyses in their raw state to literature, we forget that literature makes use of very specific signifying structures, much more granular than the structures typical of language, and, in particular, the signs of self-implication I described earlier. In fact, those signs exist only in literature and it would be impossible to find such examples in language in general.

In other words, the analysis of literature, like signifier and self-signifier, does not apply solely to the dimension of language. It is embedded in a domain of signs that are not yet verbal and, on the other hand, it is drawn out, stretched, extended toward other signs, which are much more complex than verbal signs. That is why literature is what it is only to the extent that it is not limited to the use of a single semantic surface alone, the single surface of verbal signs. In reality, literature remains upright through several thicknesses of signs. You could say it is profoundly polysemantic, but in a unique way, not in the way that a message is said to have several meanings or that it's ambiguous. In reality, literature is polysemantic, which means that, when saying one thing alone or maybe when saying nothing at all—for there is no proof that literature has to say something—in any case, whether it says something or nothing, literature is always obligated to traverse a number of semiological layers (at a minimum, the four layers I spoke of), and, in those four layers, it identifies what it needs to constitute a figure, a figure whose property is self-signification. This means that literature is nothing other than the reconfiguration, in vertical form, of the signs present in society and culture in separate layers. Literature cannot be based on silence. It is not the ineffability of silence, literature is not the effusion of that which cannot and will never be said.

In reality, literature exists only to the extent that we continue to talk about it, only to the extent that we continue to help circulate its signs. It is because it is always surrounded by signs, and because they speak, that something like literature can speak. So, very roughly schematized, this is the direction we could see a literary analysis taking, one that would be, in the strict sense of the term, semiological. It seems to me that the other approach, one with which we are both more and less familiar, would be one involving not the significant and signifying structures of the work but its spatiality.

For a long time language was considered to have had a strong relationship with time. No doubt there were several reasons for this belief. Because language is essentially what enables a story to be created and, at the same time, what allows it to promise [. . .].[8] Language is essentially that which "binds" time. And language also deposits time in itself because it is writing and, like writing, will perpetuate itself over time and perpetuate what it says over time. The surface covered with signs is, at bottom, only the spatial ruse of duration. It is, therefore, in language that time is made manifest to itself and it is also in language that it will become conscious of itself as history. And we can say that from Herder[9] to Heidegger, language as logos has always had as its major function to preserve time, to watch over it, and to perpetuate itself over time and to perpetuate time under its motionless observation.

No one, I believe, had expected that language wasn't, after all, time but space. No one, except for one man whom I do not much like but am obligated to acknowledge, and that's Bergson. Bergson had the idea that language wasn't about time but space. There was only one problem, which is that he drew a negative conclusion from this observation. And he said to himself that if language was space and not time, well then, too bad for language. And because the essence of philosophy, which, after all, is language, is to contemplate time, he drew the following two negative conclusions: first, that philosophy would have to sidestep space and language in order to be able to better conceptualize time, and, second, that to be able to conceptualize and express time, language, in some way, would have to be short-circuited; and, finally, we would have to do away with whatever was heavily spatial in language. And to neutralize these powers, or this nature, or this spatial destiny of language, language would have to be made to act against itself, to employ other words against words, counterwords, in a way; and in this fold, this shock, this intertwining of words with one another, where the spatial quality of every word would have been destroyed, in any event, wiped away, obliterated, limited by the spatial quality of other words, in this interaction, which is, in the strict sense of the term, metaphor (the importance of metaphor for Bergson stems from this), he felt that, because of this play of language against itself, because of this play of metaphor neutralizing spatialness, something would manage to come to life or, at least, to occur, and that would be the very flow of time.

In fact, what we're discovering now and by a thousand pathways that are almost all empirical is that language is space. Language is space, and we had forgotten this simply because language functions in time—it's the spoken chain—and it functions to express time. But the function of language is not its being, and the being of language, if its function is to be time, the being of language is, precisely, to be space. Space, because every element of language has meaning only within a synchronic network. Space, because the semantic value of each word or each expression is defined by the division of a table, a paradigm. Space, because the very succession of elements, the order of words, their inflections, the agreements among the different words, the length of the spoken chain, obeys, with more or less latitude, the simultaneous, architectonic, and consequently spatial, requirements of syntax. And, finally, space, because, in general, no sign signifies through a signified other than through the laws of substitution, or the combination of elements, and, therefore, through a series of determinate operations on a set—and consequently, in a space.

For a long time, almost until today I believe, the declaratory and recapitulatory functions of the sign, which are indeed temporal functions, were confused with what enables it to be a sign, and what enables a sign to be a sign is not time, it is space. God's word, because of which the signs of the end of the world are indeed the signs of the end of the world, that word does not take place in time; it can, of course, manifest itself in time, it is eternal, it is synchronic with respect to each of the signs that signify something. Literary analysis will not have any inherent meaning until it abandons all those temporal schemata in which it has been caught through the confusion of language and time. Among those schemata is the myth of creation. If criticism has, for so long, assumed the function and role of restoring this moment of initial creation, which would be the moment when the work is in the process of being born and coming to fruition, it is simply because it has obeyed the temporal mythology of language. Criticism has always had this need, this nostalgia for rediscovering the pathways of creation, of reconstituting, in its own critical discourse, the time of birth and completion which, it was believed, would hold the secrets of the work. Criticism was creationist, if you like, to the extent that its conception of language was associated with time, even to the extent that language was perceived as time: criticism believed in creation just as it believed in silence.

It seems to me that this analysis of the language of the work as space should be attempted. In fact, some people have tried it, and in several directions. I'm going to be somewhat dogmatic again and describe things that are still no more than outlines or sketches, but I'm wondering if we couldn't say, very roughly, something like the following. First, it's clear that there are spatial values associated with complex cultural configurations and which spatialize every language and every work that appears in that culture. I'm thinking, for example, of the space of the sphere from the late fifteenth century until roughly the early seventeenth century—the period that covers the very end of the Middle Ages, the Renaissance, up to the beginning of the classical period. At that time, the sphere was not simply a privileged figure in iconography or literature, one among many others; in reality, the sphere was the actually spatializing figure, the absolute, primal site in which all the other figures of Renaissance and baroque culture assumed their place. The closed curve, the center, the cupola, the radiating globe are not forms that are arbitrarily chosen by the people of that era, they are the movements by which all the possible spaces of that culture and the space of language are silently described. Empirically, of course, it was discovered that the Earth was round, which in fact highlighted the importance of the sphere; and that the Earth was the solid, dark, self-enclosed image of the celestial sphere and its vault, and the idea, as well, that man, in turn, was merely a small, microcosmic sphere placed on the cosmos of the Earth and inside the macrocosm of the ether.

Is it these discoveries, these ideas that gave the sphere its importance? Maybe it's not that important a problem. What is certain, however, and what we should be able to analyze, is the following: representation in the most general sense—image, appearance, truth, analogy—from the end of the fifteenth to the beginning of the seventeenth century, was presented in the fundamental space of the sphere. What is certain is that the pictorial cube of quatrocentro painting was replaced by the hollow half-sphere in which the figures represented by painting were placed, and displaced, by the late fifteenth and, especially, sixteenth century. What is certain is that language began to fold in on itself and invent circular forms, returning to its point of departure. For example, the fantastic voyage in *Pantagruel* culminates at its ambiguous point of departure, moving through a delightful land that evokes Olympus, Thessaly, Egypt, Libya, and, Rabelais adds, "the Hyperborean Island in the Jewish Sea." But once we've crossed this land, and having passed the islands, when we've arrived at the most distant point of our journey, when we are completely lost, this land, Rabelais goes on to say, is as graceful as the countryside of Touraine; in fact, it is this very countryside, unquestionably, the companions' point of departure, the starting point of their voyage to the islands.[10] So there was no need to make that long voyage in order to return home because they had never left it to begin with; or maybe there was no need to leave it once again because if they are already in Touraine just as they are about to re-embark, maybe it's because they are about to leave on a new voyage. In any event, the circle begins again without end.

It's probably this sphere of renascent representation, which, through its dissociation, by literally exploding, or in twisting around itself, gave us, by the mid-seventeenth century, the major baroque figures of the mirror, the iridescent bubble, the sphere, the coil, and those ample garments that twist around the body like a helix and which climb vertically. I believe we could conduct such an analysis of the spatial aspect of literary works in general, and there are a number of essays that are more than mere summaries—analyses like those of Georges Poulet, for example.[11]

It is also likely that this cultural spatiality of language in general can, strictly speaking, only grasp the work from the outside. But in fact, there also exists a spatiality within the work itself. This interior spatiality is not its composition exactly, not what we traditionally call its rhythm or its movement. In a way it's the deep space out of which and in which the figures of the work emerge and circulate. Similar analyses have been made, largely by Jean Starobinski in his book on Rousseau,[12] and by Jean Rousset[13] in *Forme et signification*. I'm thinking very specifically—and I'm merely citing the text, to which you may refer—I'm thinking of Rousset's splendid analysis of the loop and the spiral in Corneille. He shows how Corneille's dramatic works, from the *Galerie du Palais* to the *Cid,* obeyed a looping spatiality, that is, two characters are presented, who are then reunited before the beginning of the play. The play begins only to the extent that those characters become separated and, then, in the middle of the play, they meet, they meet but they cross one another, their reconciliation is impossible or imperfect. This is the story of Rodrigue and Chimène, who are unable to be completely reunited because of what has occurred. They find themselves separated once more and reunited at the end of the play. This provides the shape of the loop, a figure eight, the sign of infinity, which characterizes the spatiality of Corneille's early works. And *Polyeucte* in a way represents the eruption of an ascending movement that did not exist previously in Corneille's work. There too we find the figure eight, and two characters who are reunited before the start of the play, Polyeucte and Pauline, who are then separated, reunite, are separated once more, and are finally reunited at the end of the play. But this separation is not due to events that exist on the same plane as the characters themselves; it is the result essentially of this ascending movement caused by the conversion of Polyeucte. Another way of putting it is that the element of separation and reunion is a vertical structure that culminates in God. From that moment on, Polyeucte begins to separate from Pauline to join God, a spire that will give *Polyeucte* and Corneille's subsequent work a helical movement, the kind of ascending drapery that may be related to what we find during the same period in baroque sculpture.

Finally, a third possibility for analyzing the spatiality of the literary work may be found by studying the spatiality of the language within the work rather than the spatiality of the work in general. That means revealing a space that would not be that of culture, not that of the work, but the space of language itself, placed on the white sheet of paper, a language that, by its very nature, constitutes and opens a space, often a highly complicated space, which may ultimately have been made tangible in the work of Mallarmé—this space of innocence, of virginity, of whiteness. It is the space of the pane of glass as well, which is the space of cold, of snow, of the frost in which the bird is made captive. It is a space that is taut and smooth, that is also closed and folded back on itself.[14] It is exposed to all its qualities of licitude, it is exposed to the absolute penetration of the gaze that might scrutinize it, but the gaze can only glide over it. This open space is, at the same time, a completely enclosed space; this space we can scrutinize is a space that appears to be frozen and entirely closed. This space of Mallarméan objects, this space of the Mallarméan lake, is also the space of his words. For example, take the values that have been analyzed, rather brilliantly, by Jean-Pierre Richard,[15] the values of the fan and the wing in Mallarmé. The fan and the wing, when open, have this property of concealing from view: the wing conceals the bird from sight because of its fullness, the fan masks the face. The wing and the fan conceal from view, they hide, they provide security and remoteness, but they conceal only to the extent that they expose, that is, to the extent that we find exposed the iridescent richness of the wing or the very design of the fan. But when closed, on the contrary, the wing allows us to see the bird, the fan allows us to see the face, they allow us to approach, they allow what they recently concealed when open to be grasped by the gaze or the hand; but as soon as they are folded, they envelop, they hide everything that was exposed to view when they were open. So, the wing and the fan form the ambiguous moment of unveiling, which is the moment of enigma as well; they form the moment of the veil stretched across whatever there is to see and, also, the moment of absolute display.

This ambiguous space of Mallarméan objects, which reveals and conceals at the same time, is probably the very space of Mallarmé's words, the space of the word itself; the word, in Mallarmé, unfurls itself by enveloping, by burying what it is in the process of saying beneath this display. It is folded over the blank page, hiding what there is to say, and, in that very movement of self-concealment, brings into view, in the distance, that which remains uncompromisingly absent. And it is the movement of all Mallarmé's language probably; it is the movement, in any case, of Mallarmé's book, the book that we must approach in the most symbolic sense, with respect to the place of language, and in the most precise sense of this undertaking of Mallarmé's, in which he literally got lost at the end of his life; it is, thus, the movement of this book that, open like a fan, conceals everything it tries to reveal and when closed exposes the void he never stopped pointing out in his language. That's why the book is the very impossibility of the book: its isolating whiteness when unfurled, its revealing whiteness when closed. Mallarmé's book, in its obstinate impossibility, nearly makes visible the invisible space of language, that invisible space of language that must be analyzed, not only in Mallarmé but in every author we would want to read.

You're going to say that such possible analyses, which have been partly outlined here and there, seem to address the work in a dispersed manner. On the one hand, you have the decoding of semiological layers and, on the other hand, the analysis of forms of spatialization. Should these two movements—the analysis of semiological layers and the analysis of forms of spatialization— remain parallel? Where do they converge, or do they only converge at infinity, where the work is barely visible in its remoteness? Can we hope, one day, for a unique language that would bring into view new semiological values as well as the space in which they're spatialized?

There is absolutely no doubt that we are far from being able to have such a discussion and the disparity of the positions I've just presented is indicative of that inability.

And yet, and rather, that is certainly our task. The task of literary analysis today, the task, maybe, of philosophy, the task, maybe, of all thought and all language today would be to allow language to accommodate the space of every language, the space in which words, phonemes, sounds, written characters can, in general, be signs; one day this model, which liberates meaning while retaining language, will have to appear. But what language will have the force or the restraint, what language will have sufficient violence or neutrality to bring into view and to name the space that makes it a language? That, we don't know. Will this be a language that is much more condensed than our own, a language that does not experience the actual separation between literature, criticism, or philosophy; a language that is, in a way, absolutely primal, one that will evoke, in the strong sense of the word *evoke,* what could have been the first language of Greek thought? Or couldn't we say something else, couldn't we say that if literature actually has a meaning, and if literary analysis in the sense I've just discussed actually has a meaning, maybe it's because they presage what language will be, maybe it's because they are signs that this language is in the process of being born? After all, what is literature? Why did it appear in the nineteenth century, as I mentioned yesterday, associated with the curious space of the book? Maybe that's what literature is, in fact, this recent invention, less than two centuries old; it's fundamentally the relationship being formed, the relationship that is becoming obscurely visible but cannot yet be conceptualized, between language and space.

When language abandons what has been its age-old task, which was to gather together what should not be forgotten, when language discovers that it is connected through transgression and death to this fragment of space that is so easy to manipulate but so difficult to conceive, which is the book, then something like literature is in the process of being born. The birth of literature is still very close to us and yet, already, within its core, the question of what it is arises. It is still extremely young in a language that is very old. It has appeared in a language that for millennia, in any event since the dawn of Greek thought, has been given over to time. It has appeared, therefore, in a language given over to time, like the stammering, like the first faltering steps of a language that went on for a very long time, at the conclusion of which—and we are far from that point—that language will be given over to space. Until the nineteenth century, the book was an incidental support, the book, in its spatial materiality, was the incidental support for speech whose concern was memory and return. But the book then became—and this is where literature comes in—the book then became, roughly about the time of Sade, the essential site of language, its always repeatable origin, but ultimately without memory.

What, then, has criticism been from the time of Sainte-Beuve? What was it if not precisely the effort to think, the desperate effort, and one doomed to failure, to conceptualize in terms of time, of succession, creation, filiation, influence, something that was entirely foreign to time, something that was given over to space, which is to say, literature? And this literary analysis, practiced by so many people today, is not the promotion of criticism in a metalanguage, it is not criticism that has finally become positive, with all its small, patient gestures, with all its slightly laborious accumulations. Literary analysis, if it has any meaning, does nothing other than erase the very possibility of criticism; it gradually makes visible, but still within a fog, the fact that language is becoming increasingly less historical and successive; literary analysis shows that language is becoming increasingly distant from itself, that it is moving away from itself as a network, that its dispersion is not due to the succession of time, nor to the exhilaration of evening, but to the explosion, the brilliance, the motionless storm of midday. Literature, in the strict and serious sense of the word I've tried to explain, would be nothing other than this illuminated language, unmoving and broken, which is to say, the very thing that we now, today, need to consider.

Lectures on Sade

In March 1970, Michel Foucault was invited by the French department of the State University of New York at Buffalo to give two lectures. The first was on Flaubert's *Bouvard and Pécuchet,* the second on Sade's *La Nouvelle Justine,* a book that for Foucault was written "entirely with an eye toward truth."

The typescript for this second lecture and the various manuscripts indicate that Foucault presented his talk in two parts.[1] The first session dealt with the problem of the relationship between truth and desire in Sade. The second session anticipated the problematization that was to serve as the foundation for *The Discourse on Language* in November 1970, in particular the idea that every utterance implies a logic that obeys or, on the contrary, exposes the criteria of identification and admissibility on which the categorization and general organization of knowledge rest at a given moment in time.

Ever since *The History of Madness,* the figure of Sade—the transgressor subject to defamatory judgments and censorship; the thinker concerned with politics and truth, who condemned the justice of the ancien régime—had interested Foucault. Moreover, the "divine marquis" had been very present in the considerations of literary criticism ever since the 1960s and Foucault was not the only person to have linked Sade and Hölderlin, Mallarmé and Kafka, Lautréamont and Artaud. At the time, Sade was a kind of topos or privileged object for those who believed in a form of countermodernity.

In the fifty-three pages of the Buffalo typescript presented here, it is more the idea of a complex economy of discourse that

Foucault's internal analysis exercises. But his "use" of Sade doesn't stop there, for Foucault made him a "sergeant of sex," the promoter of a disciplinary eroticism accompanying the implementation of an instrumental rationality.[2]

In the typescript of the lecture, as in the three manuscripts, the terms "nature," "writing," "soul," and "law" are sometimes written with an initial capital and sometimes not. We have chosen to use lowercase for all these terms, restricting an initial capital to the substantive "God" to comply with current usage.

Why Did Sade Write?

||||||||||||||||||||||||||||||||||||||||||||||||||||||||||||||||||||||||||||||||||||||||||||||||||||||||||||||

I'm going to focus on one of Sade's last texts, *La Nouvelle Justine, ou les Malheurs de la vertu,* a much more fully developed version, in ten volumes, of *Justine (L'Histoire de Justine),* to which Sade added *Juliette (L'Histoire de Juliette, ou les Prospérités du vice).* The text appeared in 1797 and serves as a kind of summary, in the most extreme and most complete formulation, of Sade's thought and imagination. So it is on this text, rather than *Philosophy in the Bedroom* or *The 120 Days of Sodom,* that I would like to concentrate.

I want to add a few words of introduction to point the obvious. The entire history of *La Nouvelle Justine,* followed by the story of her sister Juliette, the entire ten volumes are positioned entirely with an eye toward truth.

In the very first line, Sade explains that, whatever disgust and horror he experiences concerning what he is about to relate, the man of letters must be sufficiently philosophical to speak the truth. And, he continues, he will show crime just as it is in actuality, that is to say, triumphant and sublime.

At the end of volume 10 (I'm skipping over all the other allusions and references he makes to the accuracy of his claim), in volume 10, in the very last lines, he again insists on the absolute truth of his novel. One of the last episodes, also one of the most astonishing, is commented on by one of the characters, who says: "No one would believe a story as improbable as this even if it appeared in a novel. But this is not a novel, it's the truth, and, therefore, you must believe me." And at the very end, in the last sentence, Sade explains that now, all the characters in the novels, Justine and Juliette, are dead, and have left behind no other narrative of their adventures than the very story that Sade has just given us; if a new author claimed to relate the adventures of Juliette and Justine, that author would be nothing more than a falsifier, would tell only lies, because Juliette and Justine are dead and they have told everything to Sade, who merely transcribed this story with the utmost accuracy, which is the real story of their lives.

I apologize for dwelling on such trivial matters. It was a tradition, in all eighteenth-century novels, to attach the narrative to some kind of truth, based on a principle of plausibility. And eighteenth-century authors very willingly made use of a variety of procedures to authenticate this kind of truth-plausibility. Sade makes use of certain rhetorical procedures that were common at that time, for example, stating something along the lines of: what I am about to relate, or what I have just related, is not the product of my imagination; I merely transcribed something that was previously written down or previously reported in a manuscript I found, or in letters that were given to me, or during a private conversation that I happened upon or overheard. I'm not the one who is speaking, but another and it's that other person who appears in the book. Consequently, what I am telling you is as true as the very existence of that person. The other method consists in the intervention of the author himself, the author who, at a given moment, speaks in his own name and says something like: this may seem improbable, but what can you do? It may have seemed improbable in a novel but not here, because I'm telling you the truth.

This type of approach, a method that was very well known in the eighteenth century and that was employed by Diderot and Sterne with great skill, was used by Sade with a carelessness and sloppiness that are extremely disconcerting. When, in *Aline et Valcour,*[1] he is supposed to be copying letters, there is a single letter that takes up an entire volume: it is almost 350 pages long and relates events that the author of the letter obviously could not have experienced—I'll skip over the details. There is a complete lack of plausibility. Similarly, when Sade himself intervenes in a note in *Justine* to say "It's true," we have to consider this statement in terms of what he's saying. In general, it occurs when a character is in the process of extolling the value of sexual excitation obtained from large-scale murder. Here, Sade can no longer contain himself and adds a small note at the bottom of the page, where he says, "I assure you it's all true; believe me, I've been completely faithful to events!" And all these various procedures used by eighteenth-century authors as methods of authentication are, in reality, in Sade's texts, merely forms of excess, repetitions, points of exasperation in the writing and, in fact, do not have the actual function of inscribing the novel within some kind of verisimilitude. To return to what I was saying, throughout his novels, Sade never stops repeating that what he is telling us is the truth. But what is this truth? Because if we follow the thread of events, it's obvious that never for a moment does the slightest verisimilitude appear in Sade's text: the thousands of deaths, the massacres that occur throughout the course of the day, the young men and women who are butchered once endlessly renewed forms of sexual enjoyment have been obtained from them; someone who, with a single blow, destroys twenty-four hospitals and the fifteen thousand persons who occupy them, in Rome; someone who provokes a volcanic eruption. Such techniques are common practice in Sade's text and Sade, again, continues to repeat: "What I have just told you is the truth."

So, what is this truth? This truth that is no way comparable to the truth-plausibility of eighteenth-century novelists, this truth that can in no way be taken literally when we consider the actual contents of the story. Well, the truth Sade speaks of, quite simply, is not really the truth of what he's narrating, it's the truth of his reasoning. The problem, for the eighteenth-century novelist, was to establish, in the form of plausibility, a fiction capable of moving us; Sade's problem is to demonstrate a truth—to demonstrate a truth as a philosopher, not to demonstrate a truth that is absolutely tied to the creation of desire.

In *Justine,* it is a question of bringing about, in the exercise of desire, in the exercise of domination, savagery, and murder, something that is true; and what the characters say at the very moment when they are in the process of carrying out these acts, or what they say afterwards or before to explain or justify them, that's what must be true. In other words, what must be true is the reasoning process, it's this form of rationality promoted by the exercise of desire or that supports the exercise of desire. Sade is constantly telling us this throughout the text, telling us that it's the truth itself. This is what I think we must establish in order to correctly frame the problem of the relationship between truth and desire in Sade.

So how do these relationships between truth and desire manifest themselves, in what form and on what level? I believe we can analyze them in two ways, on two levels: first, through the very existence of the book; second, in the content of the arguments put forth by the characters.

It's this first question I'd like to discuss this evening: the existence of the book. The problem is simple. Why did Sade write? What did the practice of writing mean for Sade? We know from his biography that he wrote thousands of pages, far more than what is found in the texts that have been preserved, and even those are vast. He lost a considerable amount of work during his various imprisonments, because they were confiscated as quickly as he wrote them on small scraps of paper. When he wrote the *120 Days [of Sodom]* in the Bastille (I believe this was completed in 1788–1789), the papers were taken from him as soon as the Bastille fell. The downside of the fall of the Bastille was the disappearance of *120 Days [of Sodom]*. Fortunately, it was rediscovered, but after Sade's death; which didn't prevent Sade from weeping "tears of blood." He wept such tears because he had lost his text. All of this, Sade's obstinacy in writing, the fact of his weeping tears of blood when he lost a text, added to the fact that whenever he published something (well, not every time, but several times, when he managed to publish his work), he was imprisoned. This proves that Sade attributed considerable importance to writing. And by writing, we shouldn't understand this to mean the act of writing alone but that of publishing, because he published his texts and if chance would have it that he was not in prison at the moment of their publication, he was immediately returned to prison because of those publications.

Why was writing so important to Sade? I believe that, at first glance, the importance of writing for him was—and he said this on several occasions in *Justine* and *Juliette*—that he addressed his readers not because of the pleasure they might obtain from his stories but in spite of the disagreeableness they might find in his novels. He said: "You will not be pleased to hear such terrible stories. Virtue always punished, vice always rewarded, children massacred, young men and women cut into pieces, pregnant women hung, entire hospitals burned, this," Sade said, "is not very pleasant to listen to. Your sensibility is going to be revolted, your heart will feel like it's going to burst, but what do you expect? I'm not addressing your sensibility or your heart, but your reason and your reason alone. I want to demonstrate a fundamental truth, which is that vice is always rewarded and virtue always punished." However, a problem arises, which is that, when following one of Sade's novels, we find that there is absolutely no logic to the rewarding of vice and the punishment of virtue. In fact, whenever Justine, who is virtuous, is punished, the punishment is never due to the fact that Justine has committed a fault of reasoning, has failed to anticipate something, has been blind to some reality. In fact, Justine's calculations are perfect, but some terrifying misfortune always occurs, which has something of the arbitrary and accidental, because of which she will be punished. Justine saves someone and, at the very moment she does so, someone else passes by who kills the person whose life she has just saved, carries Justine off to a hideout for thieves or counterfeiters, and so on. It is always chance that intervenes, it is never the logical consequence of someone's acts that determines their punishment.

On the other hand, in *Juliette,* the same thing occurs: the upstanding Juliette commits the most horrible crimes. And finally she herself encounters someone who appears to be more of a criminal than herself, a hideous Italian bandit known as Bras-de-Fer. Assuming an Italian could call himself Bras-de-Fer. She is to be condemned to death, but what will enable her to escape death? The accuracy of her calculations? Her intellect? Her lucidity? Not at all. Quite simply, the fact that Bras-de-Fer is both the brother and the husband of her good friend, Clairvil, whom Juliette knew in the past; consequently, everything works out and Juliette is not condemned. The fact that vice has prospered on this occasion is in no way associated with the logical consequence of her behavior but simply with chance. Therefore, it is Sade himself who has arranged a system of intersections, arbitrary events. He has arranged them in such a way that in his story, it is always vice that is rewarded and virtue that is always punished. But if we were to distribute the events in a different manner, we would have the same results. Therefore, it is absolutely not the rationality of vice or virtue that is in question, so that when Sade says, "I'm not addressing your heart but your reason," he's obviously taking us for a ride and not really taking himself seriously.

So what is Sade doing when he claims to advance this proof, when he claims to address our reason, while in fact the entire framework of the story is addressed to something else entirely?

I believe that to fully understand the function of writing in Sade, we need to examine the following excerpt. I believe it's the only passage in *Justine* and *Juliette* that relates to the activity of writing. Here we have Juliette herself addressing a character, one of her friends and already quite perverse, but not yet quite perverse enough. It is a question of her last apprenticeship, of taking the last step toward perversion. And this is how Juliette advises her:

> Go a whole fortnight without lewd occupations, divert yourself, amuse yourself at other things; for the space of those two weeks rigorously bar every libertine thought from your mind. At the close of the final day retire alone to your bed, calmly and in silence; lying there, summon up all those images and ideas you banished during the fasting period just elapsed, and indolently, languidly, nonchalantly fall to performing that wanton little pollution by which nobody so cunningly arouses herself or others as do you. Next, unpent your fancy, let it freely dwell upon aberrations of different sorts and of ascending magnitude; linger over the details of each, pass them all one by one in review; assure yourself that you are absolute sovereign in a world groveling at your feet, that yours is the supreme and unchallengeable right to change, mutilate, destroy, annihilate any and all the living beings you like. Fear of reprisals, hindrances you have none: choose what pleases you, but leave nothing out, make no exceptions; show consideration to no one whomsoever, sever every hobbling tie, abolish every check, let nothing stand in your way; leave everything to your imagination, let it pursue its bent and content yourself to follow in its train, above all avoiding any precipitate gesture: let it be your head and not your temperament that commands your fingers. Without your noticing it, from among all the various scenes you visualize one will claim your attention more energetically than the others and will so forcefully rivet itself in your mind that you'll be unable to dislodge it or supplant it by another. The idea,

acquired by the means I am outlining, will dominate you, captivate you; delirium will invade your senses, and thinking yourself actually at work, you will discharge like a Messalina. Once this is accomplished, light your bedside lamp and write out a full description of the abomination which has just inflamed you, omitting nothing that could serve to aggravate its details; and then go to sleep thinking about them. Reread your notes the next day and, as you recommence your operation, add everything your imagination, doubtless a bit weary by now of an idea which has already cost you fuck, may suggest that could heighten its power to exacerbate. Now turn to the definitive shaping of this idea into a scheme and as you put the final touches on it, once again incorporate all fresh episodes, novelties, and ramifications that occur to you. After that, execute it, and you will find that this is the species of viciousness which suits you best and which you will carry out with the greatest delight. My formula, I am aware, has its wicked side but it is infallible, and I would not recommend it to you if I had not tested it successfully.[2]

The passage clearly shows a use of writing, one that is, in fact, perfectly clear. Typically, it involves a method of masturbation. We start from the complete freedom given to the imagination; this results in a first release. We fall asleep and reread; there ensues a new effort of imagination, new elaboration in writing, and then, as Sade says, almost like a kitchen recipe: "Execute it . . ." Concerning the text, there are three things I would like to point out. First, writing, far from being the instrument of rational communication Sade speaks of elsewhere (when he claims, "When I write, I'm not addressing your senses, your imagination, or your heart, but simply your head, and in order to convince you"), far from being the instrument of universal rationality, appears, purely and simply, as an instrument, an additive, an aid to individual fantasy. It's a way of combining an erotic reverie with sexual practice. And it is clearly stated in the text that this is a purely individual recipe, because it should result in an alteration that is most suitable for you personally. Consequently, in constructing a fantasy, in developing a sexual practice, writing is simply one step leading from imagination to practice.

Second, we see that it's very likely that this recipe for writing fantasy, for purely erotic writing, it's highly likely that Sade himself experimented with it and, given this likelihood, this is the way he actually wrote his novels. What Juliette explains in this passage is probably the procedure Sade followed during the forty years of his reclusion, something he did every morning and every evening, except for its realization, of course: the writing he describes here is the writing of his own books, it's the writing of his solitary frenzy.

Third, this description of the role of writing can be found, transferred but very faithfully reproduced, in a text that was absolutely public, not banned, known as *Reflections on the Novel [Idées sur le roman]*. In this text, Sade says (thereby authenticating the text and his own practice of writing) that the novelist must proceed in the following manner: the good novelist must plunge into nature the way his mother's lover would plunge into the body of his mother. The novelist is, therefore, the incestuous son of nature, he gives himself to his mother-nature just as the character in the novel gives herself over to the imagination. The novelist, once he has plunged into the bosom of nature, will write and as he writes, Sade says, he will crack open the breast that was offered to him. Here, once more, the sexual imagery is obvious. At that moment, he says, having penetrated, having opened the breast, the novelist must no longer control himself, must not allow himself to be constrained by any barrier. And addressing the writer, Sade says, "Let no barrier restrain you; exercise at will your right to attack or take liberties with any and all of history's anecdotes, whenever the rupture of this restriction demands it in the formation of the pleasures you are preparing for us."[3] Consequently, nature offers truths, a history; it provides the elements as a mother who gives pleasure to her child, but the novelist must systematically vary those elements, must deform them, must feel he is the absolute master, exactly as in the description I've just read, based on this general imagination, maternal and incestuous, which he is endowed with from the start. The libertine exercises his imagination by varying and multiplying the images he presents. Then, *Reflections on the Novel* continues, you will produce a sketch and this sketch, once set down on paper, you must work hard to expand, but without restricting yourself to the limits it may appear to dictate to you; go beyond your initial intentions, vary them, augment them. You find, in this passage from *Reflections on the Novel,* the equivalent of what occurs in sexual fantasy, for once the sketch has been set down, it involves taking it up again, reworking it, allowing the imagination to do its work on the writing, just as, the morning after the fantasy, we return to the text that we had written, reread it, and write it once more, adding all the details that present themselves to our imagination. And the text of *Reflections on the Novel* concludes as follows: "All I ask of you is this one thing, sustain interest throughout, to the very last page."[4]

Here you see that the last page plays the role that reality played in the text I spoke of earlier. In other words, the two descriptions of writing, the description of dreamlike writing we find here and the advice to writers Sade provides in *Reflections on the Novel,* are absolutely symmetrical. The procedures are the same, the only two elements that vary are the following: initially, in Juliette's reverie, what is given is the freedom of the imagination; in the case of *Reflections on the Novel,* it is nature. The second element that varies, in the end, in the case of Juliette's reverie, is reality ("After that, execute it," Sade writes); and in the case of *Reflections on the Novel,* he says that this is how we reach the final page. But aside from these two differences, to which I'll return, both methods are the same, and the way in which Sade tells us how to write novels, the way in which he appears to have written his own novels, coincides with his recommendation for using writing for the purpose of sexual fantasy. Therefore, we should have no illusions about this; it's quite clear that for Sade writing is not at all what it is purported to be in his novel, it is not at all something reasonable that, starting from reason, addresses the reason of readers; it is something else entirely. For Sade, writing is sexual fantasy and, in that sense, we again encounter the question: what relationship can it have with truth? How can we claim to tell the truth if all we are doing is transcribing onto paper what are purely and simply sexual fantasies? Isn't Sade mistaken, isn't he deceiving us when, toying with his writing the way he toys with his imagination or, rather, toying with his writing so he can better exercise his imagination, he has the audacity or lack of awareness to tell us that he's telling the truth?

We need to take a closer look at the passage I've just read. We need to ask exactly how writing functions in this text.

First, writing here serves as an intermediary element between the imaginary and the real. Sade, or the character in question, from the outset offers the totality of the imaginary world possible: he varies this imaginary world, exceeds its limits, disturbs its borders; he will even go beyond it, although he thought he had already imagined all that could be imagined, and it is this that he will retranscribe repeatedly. Only when he has copied it out, only when he has transcribed it, will he arrive at reality and his bold recommendation, "After that, execute it," as if this were a simple matter when we've dreamt of slaughtering ten thousand children, burned hundreds of hospitals, caused a volcano to explode, and so on. Writing, then, is this method, this moment that will lead to the real but which, in truth, pushes the real to the limits of nonexistence. Writing extends the imagination, enables us to multiply it, to cross borders, and it will reduce the real to this insignificance that is indicated in the text as "After that, execute it." Writing will, in a way, enable us to push the reality principle as far from the borders of the imagination as possible; writing is that which possesses the force to push the moment of understanding away, to always shift it beyond the imagination; it is writing that has the strength to work the imagination and delay the moment of the real, and will finally substitute itself for the reality principle. Through writing, the imaginary will no longer have to take the step that until then had been absolutely indispensable, the step toward reality. Writing will reject reality until it is as unreal as the imagination itself; writing is that which takes the place of the reality principle and absolves the imagination from ever having to achieve reality.

The first function of writing, therefore, is to abolish the barrier between reality and imagination. Writing is that which excludes reality; consequently, it is that which will free up, will remove every limit to the imaginary itself. Because of writing, we will have, to use Freudian vocabulary, a world entirely governed by the pleasure principle that will never have to encounter the reality principle.

Second, again referring to this same text, we note that this writing is situated very precisely between two moments of sexual enjoyment. It says quite clearly that the movement of the imagination must be guided carefully and gradually up to the first instance of sexual release and that it is only after this that we will write. Then we'll go to sleep calmly and the next morning resume our reading, and, Sade says, everything can begin again, the writing here playing the role within the sexual fantasy of a repetition principle. That is to say that because of writing, because of the thing written, we'll be able to return to what we dreamt, we'll be able to repeat it in our imagination, and, by repeating it in our imagination, we'll be able to obtain from this repeated imagination the repetition of what had already occurred, which is sexual release.

Writing is the principle of repeated enjoyment; writing is what delights or enables us to repeat. The hedonism of writing and writing as repeated delight are thereby marked. Sade provides the principle and the most radical, the most brazen sexual root for everything that, traditionally, in the classical literary theory of the eighteenth century, characterized the literary principle of increasing interest, the fact that things are narrated in such a way that our interest is always maintained, namely, writing as the principle of perpetually renewed sexual release. Writing will serve to erase the limitation of time, it will enable the limits of exhaustion, fatigue, old age, and death to be wiped away. Through writing, everything will be able to begin again perpetually, indefinitely; fatigue, exhaustion, death will never appear in this world of writing. As we saw earlier, writing is that which eliminates the difference between the pleasure principle and the reality principle. The second function of writing, therefore, is to erase the limitations of time and free repetition for itself. We are in the very world of repetition and that is why, throughout Sade's novels, we find the same stories repeated ad infinitum, the same characters, the same gestures, the same acts, the same violence, the same discourse as well, and the same reasoning, since it is precisely in this world of writing that temporal limits vanish. At the end of the history of Juliette, the final volume concludes with these words: "The company left the following morning; greatest success crowned our heroes for the next ten years."[5] And then Juliette disappears from the world, no one knows how; although she has no reason to disappear because, after all, we're in the world of repetition; everything must be repeated indefinitely and there is no way that Juliette can really die.

Third, the role of writing, if we continue to follow Sade's text, is not simply to introduce the indefinite repetition of pleasure, it is also to exceed, to enable the imagination to exceed its own limits: "Once this is accomplished, light your bedside lamp and write out a full description of the abomination which has just inflamed you, omitting nothing that could serve to aggravate its details; and then go to sleep thinking about them. Reread your notes the next day and, as you recommence your operation, add everything your imagination, doubtless a bit weary by now of an idea which has already cost you fuck, may suggest that could heighten its power to exacerbate."

Consequently, repetitive writing is also multiplicative writing, writing that exacerbates, writing that augments and multiplies without end. This rewriting, this writing–reading–rewriting– rereading and so on, helps push the imagination always further; every time we write we prepare to exceed new limits. Writing exposes and is witness to the opening up of an infinite space before it in which images, pleasures, and excess are multiplied without limit. Thus, writing, which is the unlimitedness of plea- sure with respect to reality, the unlimitedness of repetition with respect to time, is at the same time the unlimitedness of the image itself; it is the unlimitedness of the limit itself because all limits, one by one, are exceeded. No image is stabilized once and for all, desire is never captured in a fantasy; there is always another fantasy behind the fantasy and, therefore, it is also the elimination of the very limits of fantasy that writing provides.

The fourth function of literature is expressed by the text itself: "After that, execute it, and you will find that this is the species of viciousness which suits you best and which you will carry out with the greatest delight." That is to say, through this method by which writing leads to the unlimited release of fantasy, unlimited repetition in time, it enables the individual to obtain, compared to other individuals, compared to behavioral norms and habits, compared to all laws, to everything that is permitted and for- bidden, the maximum excess possible, the maximum distance possible. The imagined act, developed through writing, pushed as far as it can go, pushed beyond even those limits, this act, whether executed or not, matters little because writing no longer provides a pertinent difference; the act will position the individual at a point of the impossible such that he will now be at the most deviant point of all singularity, he will achieve the maximum excess possible, he will have nothing whatsoever in common with anyone. As the engine of this movement, writing is the principle of excess and extremity, it positions the individual not only in a singularity but in an irremediable solitude. From that moment—and Sade will reiterate this in several other texts—when the subject, the individual, has conceived this absolutely abominable or impossible act, when he has actually carried it out, he can no longer turn back: no remorse, no regret, no recovery is possible. Once the act is committed, the individual is absolutely and totally criminal; nothing will eradicate the existence of the crime, nothing will eradicate the individual as crime. Writing is, therefore, the principle by which and, in any case, through which the criminal will be established as a criminal. Writing establishes the final excess and from that moment on, from the moment it places the individual at this extreme point, can we still effectively speak of crime? If there is no remorse, if there is no way the individual can make up for the crime he has committed, if no punishment can really affect him, if his conscience does not recognize the act as criminal, at that moment, the crime itself is obliterated and the individual suddenly appears, to himself and to others, not as a criminal who has broken laws but simply as an absolutely singular individual, as someone unique, having no relation to others, and the crime is expunged to the benefit of a notion central to Sade: irregularity.

In this way, writing, which has already eliminated several limits, now removes this final limit, which is the limit between the criminal and the noncriminal, between what is permitted and what is not, and introduces irregularity into the uncertain world. We can now better comprehend what Sade wants to express when he writes: "I write to tell the truth." For Sade, telling the truth obviously does not mean saying something probable, similar to eighteenth-century novelists, this much we've already established. For Sade, telling the truth means establishing desire, fantasy, erotic imagination in a relationship to truth that is such that there will be no reality principle capable of opposing that desire, capable of saying no, capable of saying, "There are things you will not accomplish," capable of saying, "You're mistaken, you are merely fantasy and imagination." From the moment that writing, fully compliant with desire, exercises that desire, multiplies it, rejects the reality principle, suddenly, corroboration of the fantasy is no longer possible. This means that every fantasy becomes true and the imagination itself becomes its own corroboration; rather, the only corroboration possible is the fact of surpassing one fantasy and discovering another.

Second, writing will introduce desire into the order of truth for, to the extent that writing allows us to obliterate all temporal limits and, consequently, to introduce desire into the eternal world of repetition, desire is not something that exists at a given moment only to disappear. Through writing, desire is no longer something that, existing at a given moment and being true at that moment, will subsequently be false; it is not something that will be revealed to be chimerical at the end of life and at the moment of death because there is no longer any death, because there is no end to life, because we are perpetually engaged in repetition. And suddenly, the suppression of this temporal barrier, the inception of a world of repetition, means that desire will always be true and that nothing can ever invalidate it.

Third, writing introduces desire into the world of truth because it erases every limit to desire and every limit of the licit and the illicit, of the permitted and the not-permitted, of the moral and the immoral. That is to say, writing introduces desire into the space of the indefinitely possible and always unlimited possible. Writing enables imagination and desire to avoid ever having to encounter anything other than their own unique individuality.

In a way, it allows desire to always be adequate to its own irregularity; nothing can ever repress or contain it; desire is always on a firm footing with its own truth. Because of all this illimitability, produced by the fact of writing, desire will itself become its own law; it will become an absolute sovereign embodying its own truth, its own repetition, its own infinity, its own means of verification. Nothing can any longer say to desire, "You are false." Nothing can any longer say to desire, "You are not the totality." Nothing can any longer say to desire, "Your dreams exist but you do not go unopposed." Nothing can any longer say to desire, "You experience this but reality presents you with something else." Through writing, desire has become, has entered the world of total, absolute, and unlimited truth, once and for all, a truth without any possible external challenge.

To this extent, we find that Sadean literature is not at all characterized by the idea of communicating, of imposing, of suggesting another's ideas or sentiments; it is not at all concerned with persuading someone of an external truth. Sadean writing is one that, in reality, is addressed to no one, and it is addressed to no one to the extent that it has no concern whatsoever with persuading someone of a truth that Sade might have in mind or might have perceived or recognized, and would be self-evident, would be self-evident for reader and author alike. Sade's writing is an absolutely solitary writing that, in a sense, no one can understand and no one can be persuaded by. And yet, it is absolutely imperative for Sade that these fantasies are expressed in writing, through whatever materiality it has, through whatever solidity it has, because, as with the text of *Juliette,* it is this writing, this material writing, this writing made of signs placed on a page we can read, correct, and revise indefinitely, it is this writing that will inject desire into the completely unlimited space where the external, time, the limits of the imagination, defenses, and permissions are completely eliminated once and for all. Writing then becomes simply desire that has finally achieved a truth that nothing can limit. Writing is desire become truth, it is truth that has taken the form of desire, of repetitive desire, unlimited desire, desire without law, without restriction, without an exterior, and it is the suppression of exteriority with respect to desire. No doubt this is what writing effectively accomplishes in the work of Sade, and that is why Sade writes.

Theoretical Discourses and Erotic Scenes

||||||||||||||||||||||||||||||||||||||||||||||||||||||||||||||||||||||||||||||||||||||||||||||||||||||||||||||||

We have just examined Sade's reasons for using and recording his fantasies, and the relationship between erotic desire, fantasy, reverie, and phantasmagoria in his writing. We're now going to shift the analysis slightly and investigate the meaning Sade gives not so much to his theoretical discourses but to the alternation we find throughout Sade's writing between theoretical discourses and erotic scenes. (I'll call "scenes" those passages in which Sade explains and describes the sexual configurations enacted by the partners and characters in his novels, and "discourses" those lengthy theoretical passages that are regularly interspersed, with the exactitude of a balance, with the erotic scenes.) In any event, it is this problem I would like to address first, that is, the alternation between discourse and scene. Not only is this alternation visible, it is obsessional because every scene, with mechanical regularity, is preceded by a theoretical discourse that is, in turn, followed by a scene and this continues throughout the ten volumes of *Justine* and *Juliette.*[1] In *The 120 Days of Sodom,* the mechanism is organized in advance because certain times of the day are very explicitly set aside for discourse while others are reserved for erotic scenes. What does this principle of alternation signify? That's the topic I'd like to examine now.

The first idea or explanation that comes to mind is, obviously, quite simple. After all, aren't these theoretical passages that alternate with the erotic scene there to express the truth of those erotic scenes? The scenes would represent things, acts;

the practices would represent the dramaturgy, the theater of sexuality; and the discourses would explain—before or after—what has occurred, in order to express the truth, to show, to justify what has been presented in the previous or following passages. Yet, what is really striking when we begin to examine these discourse elements is that Sade never explains, never tries to explain what sexuality is; how it is, for example, that we can desire our own mother, or how it is that we can be homosexual, or why someone has a desire to kill small children, and so on. Finally, anything that could, in terms of psychology or physiology, or simply a naturalist explanation, account for what is actually narrated, anything that might express, in terms of truthful explanation, what has been presented in the form of a scene, is never found in Sade's discourses. These discourses do not speak about desire, nor do they speak about sexuality; sexuality and desire are not the subject of the discourses. The subject of Sade's discourse is something else; it is the question of God, of laws, of the social contract, of crime in general; it is the question of nature, the soul, immortality, eternity. These are the subjects we find in Sadean discourse; desire is not present in these discourses as a subject. On the other hand—and this second comment, when compared with the first, will serve as our starting point—there exists between desire, which is not present as a subject in the discourse, and the discourse itself, there exists an obvious connection, which is quasi-physiological, because Sade's discourse takes place either before or after the scene. When it occurs before the scene, the discourse serves in a way to construct the theater in which the scene will unfold. For example, at the end of *Juliette,* he describes the rape of little Fontange, a young girl entrusted to Juliette, whom Juliette robs of her financial assets, before stripping her of her clothing, raping and killing her. Before the scene, there is a lengthy discourse on the social contract, on the relations of obligation that can exist between individuals and on the relatively restrictive nature of the obligation that can bind individuals to one another. In a way, it's the theoretical theater in which the scene will take place because little Fontange has been given by her mother to Juliette, who has promised to look after her, to preserve her wealth, and arrange her marriage, all of which she obviously does not do. Yet, at the end of this lengthy discourse, which is a theoretical staging of what is about to transpire, of the drama that is about to take place, what happens? By the very fact of this discourse—in which the discussion focuses only on obligation in general, the duties of reciprocity, contracts, legislation, criminality, and so on—at the conclusion of this purely theoretical discourse, the partners to the discussion, those who are in the process of debating these subjects, have reached such an intense state of sexual excitement, by the fact of this theoretical discussion alone, that they naturally enact what is about to occur (none of which was contemplated during the discourse because the discourse was entirely abstract, focusing on the law and other matters, and this was sufficient to lead them to the highest pitch of sexual excitement).

In other episodes, the discourse does not precede the scene, it follows it. Something happens (Bressac rapes his mother) and a discourse is presented to explain it; for example, why and how family relationships should not be taken seriously and lengthy considerations on the family at the conclusion of which people are once again, and by the sole fact of this theoretical discourse, brought to a peak of sexual excitement such that they are unable to avoid repeating what they have already enacted, such that the discourse functions as the engine and principle of desire. In a sense it is connected to desire on the mechanical level; the mechanics of the discourse bring about the mechanics of desire, and when the mechanism has come to an end, the discourse takes over and sets desire in motion again, so that desire and discourse are connected to each other through their internal mechanism, whereas desire itself is not present in the discourse. Sade's discourse, therefore, is not a discourse about desire; it's a discourse with desire, a discourse in the wake of desire, a discourse before or after desire, a discourse that takes the place of desire before desire appears on the scene or after desire has disappeared; discourse is a substitute for desire. Discourse and desire thus have the same place and, consequently, trigger each other, without discourse being superior to desire in expressing the truth. It is this topic, namely, the fact that discourse does not speak the truth about desire but that discourse and desire are connected to each other, that truth and desire are connected to each other according to a given mechanism. It is this topic I'd like to develop.

So, the first question is: what do we find in these discourses? What do they tell us? Basically, they always say the same thing. Sade's discourses say exactly the same thing, well, not the same thing but the same four things. The discourses, throughout the ten volumes of *Justine* and *Juliette* as well as *The 120 Days of Sodom,* and all of Sade's other works, say the same four things. It's like a four-sided polyhedron that is continuously tossed by the characters and that lands, sometimes on one face and sometimes on another or, throughout a discourse, might roll successively on each of the four faces, those four faces being easy to determine. Each bears an acknowledgment of nonexistence.

The first face, the base of this polyhedron, of course, is the following: God does not exist and the proof that God does not exist is that he is completely contradictory. We claim that God is omnipotent, but how is it that at every moment his will can be counterbalanced by the will of men? Therefore, he is impotent. It is said that God is free, but, in fact, men are free not to do what God wishes; therefore, God is not free! It is said that God is good, but it is sufficient to look at the world as it exists to see that God is not good but cruel. And, therefore, God does not exist because he is contradictory. That is our first conclusion.

Our second conclusion is that the soul also does not exist because it is contradictory. If it is bound to the body, if it is subject to the body, if it can be invaded by desire or emotion, it is material. If it is born with the body, if it appears in the world at the same time as the body, it is material. If it is born with the body, if it appears in the world at the same time as the body, it is not eternal as is claimed and, therefore, is perishable. If the soul is guilty when it has sinned, how can this sin be pardoned one day and the soul return to innocence? On the other hand, if the soul is determined to behave as it does, how can it be condemned? And so on. There follows a series of paradoxes, all of which tend to demonstrate that the soul is inherently contradictory and, consequently, cannot exist.

The third conclusion of nonexistence is that crime does not exist. Crime exists only in relation to the law; where there is no law, there is no crime. When the law does not proscribe something, that something cannot exist as a crime. But what is the law other than what has been decided by certain individuals for their own benefit? What is the law other than the expression of a conspiracy of certain individuals to foster their own interest and, consequently, how can we say that crime is evil if it is simply that which is opposed to the will of certain individuals and, at most, to their hypocrisy?

The fourth conclusion again relates to nonexistence: nature does not exist; rather, nature exists, but if it exists, it exists only in the form of destruction and, as a result, the suppression of itself. What, in fact, is nature? Nature is that which produces living beings. And what characterizes living beings other than that they die? And they die either through some natural fatality, which occurs when they grow old, which demonstrates that nature can do nothing other than destroy itself; or death occurs through the violence of other individuals, who have themselves been created by nature along with their violence, their cruelty, their appetites, their anthropophagy, and so on. Once again it is nature that destroys itself; therefore, nature is always self-destruction, and yet the nature of each individual is such that he strives to preserve himself. And nature has introduced this need of preservation in every individual. However, if self-preservation is a law of nature, how is it that it's also a law of nature that individuals die, die by their own hand or that of others? Therefore, we find, in the need of beings for self-preservation and in the fatality that condemns them to die, something that embeds a contradiction within the very heart of nature, through which nature itself disappears.

So we have four propositions of nonexistence: God does not exist, the soul does not exist, crime does not exist, and nature does not exist, and it is these four propositions that, in all their variety and with all their consequences and assumptions, are continuously repeated throughout Sade's work. Yet these four propositions exactly define what could be called irregular existence for Sade. What is an irregular individual in Sade's sense? It is someone who, once and for all, presents the quadruple principle of this quadruple nonexistence; it is an individual who recognizes no sovereignty above himself: not God, not the soul, not the law, not nature. It is an individual who is at no time connected to any eternity, any immortality, any obligation, any continuity, and who would surpass not only the moment of his life but of his desire. Irregular existence is an existence that recognizes no norm, not a religious norm derived from God, not a personal norm defined by the soul, not a social norm defined by crime, not a natural norm. Lastly, irregular existence is an existence that does not recognize any impossibility. If there is no God, no personal identity, no nature, no human constraint derived from a society or a law, then there is no longer any difference between the possible and the impossible. Ultimately, irregular existence, which is to say, Juliette's existence, the existence of the Sadean hero, is an existence in which anything can occur outside these norms, wherein all moments can be discontinuously resumed.

This, then, is the first thing we find in these discourses, whose four negative propositions define the irregular existence of the Sadean personality.

On this basis we can try to ask how these discourses function. What purpose do they serve? Why these discourses with their four negative propositions? Why do they occur? What role do they play and how are they related to desire by this mechanism in which the sexual excitement of the characters at the conclusion of the discourses is both effect and symbol? As a kind of hypothesis, I would like to reframe, to isolate, five functions of these Sadean discourses.

The first function is clear, obvious, meaningful. The discourses occur before the orgy scenes, before the debauchery, before the crimes. Why? So that the characters do not turn back on their desires, on any of their desires, and so they do not allow any of the objects they seek to escape. The discourses, in the context of this first function, serve first, to abolish all limits, to erase every limit desire might encounter, so that no desire is relinquished; second, to create a situation in which one never sacrifices one's own interests and, consequently, never sacrifices oneself for the benefit of the other. In other words, my desires must be completely satisfied; my interest must always come first; and my existence must be saved absolutely. This is what the Sadean character repeats before beginning the orgy scene, it is what he repeats to himself, it is what he says to the other to convince him and draw him forward: "You will not abandon any of your desires, you will not sacrifice your own self-interest in any way, you will always consider your life to be absolute." If we examine this first, very simple and very obvious function of the discourse, we see that the discourse, which is presented as a philosophical discourse, as a lengthy demonstration of four nonexistences, we see that the discourse is really quite astonishing because, at bottom, it is the reversal, term by term, of the function of the philosophical, ideological discourse of the West.

In the West, discourse, or ideological discourse, played a castrating role. Ever since Plato, it involved defining, establishing the identity of the individual on the basis of the renunciation of a part of himself. Philosophical and religious discourse has operated like this ever since classical Greece: you will be fully yourself only to the extent that you renounce a part of yourself. Therefore, you will be recognized by God, you will be named by him, you will be called by him, you will be eternally chosen by him to become one of the elect; eternity will pronounce your name only if you renounce the world, the body, time, desire. This same religious and philosophical discourse of the West goes on to say that you will have a place in society, you will be recognized among the rest of your kind, you will receive a name, a unique name, and consequently will escape the collective qualification of criminal or madman; you will have a name and renown only to the extent that you exist individually and, therefore, only to the extent that you renounce your desires, your murderous impulses, your fantasies, your body, and the law of your body. Philosophical and religious discourse, theological discourse, is a castrating discourse and, compared to it, we can say that Sadean discourse has a de-castrating function to the extent that it entails not surpassing the moment of castration but negating, denying, and rejecting castration itself. And it does this by a very simple shifting maneuver in its negations: Sadean discourse negates everything that philosophical and religious discourse had tried to acknowledge. The West's religious and philosophical discourse has always, in one way or another, affirmed God, affirmed the soul, affirmed the law, affirmed nature. Sadean discourse denies all that. Conversely, Western philosophical discourse, beginning with these four fundamental affirmations, this four-part philosophical assertion, had introduced the negative aspect of these obligations: because your soul exists, you do not have the right to do this; because there is a law, you will renounce this thing; because nature exists, you must not violate it. In other words, Western philosophical discourse, starting with these four fundamental assertions, these four fundamental affirmations, introduced negation into the moral order, the order of the law, the prescriptive order. Western metaphysics is affirmative at the level of ontology; it is negative at the level of prescriptiveness. Conversely, the function of Sadean discourse is to reverse the negation, to negate everything that had been affirmed: God does not exist. Therefore, nature does not exist, the law does not exist, the soul does not exist, and, consequently, everything is possible and nothing will be denied any longer by the prescriptive order.

To summarize, we could say there are four types of discourse. First, there is the discourse of the unconscious, if we are to believe Freud, which is entirely affirmative. It asserts that things exist while simultaneously asserting that desire desires; thus, two assertions at the level of existence and desire. At the other extremity, you have schizophrenic discourse, which denies everything. Nothing exists (the world does not exist, nature does not exist, I do not exist, others do not exist) and this negation surrounds the negation of desire: I desire nothing. So, you have the discourse of the unconscious, which is entirely affirmative, and the schizophrenic discourse, which is entirely negative. There is ideological, or philosophical, or religious discourse, which asserts in the order of truth (God, nature, the world, and the soul exist) and denies in the order of desire—"therefore, you shall not desire, therefore, you shall renounce." And then, you have the fourth discourse, the libertine discourse, which is the reverse of ideological discourse, and which we could also refer to as perverse discourse. It is the discourse that denies everything that philosophical discourse affirms, and which, therefore, denies in the order of assertion and affirms in the order of prescriptiveness, and says: God does not exist, the soul does not

exist, nature does not exist, therefore, I desire. And the first function of this form of discourse is to establish itself as libertine
discourse, that is to say, a discourse that shifts the system of
negation to within the metaphysical discourse of the West, the
discourse that, with respect to desire, plays the significant function of castration.

The second function of Sadean discourse is the following:
in all of Sade's texts libertine discourse is obviously promoted
by Sade's positive hero, that is, the libertine himself. But, with
respect not so much to the speaker but the person to whom this
speech is addressed, the interlocutor, on several occasions the
interlocutor is simply the future victim. The future victim is told:
God does not exist and if you accept this truth, you will escape
your suffering. But what is strange is that no victim is ever persuaded and all of them, notwithstanding the obvious threat that
weighs upon them, remain completely unmoved by these arguments. Yet, the discourse is presented by Sade as one that is not
only absolutely truthful with respect to its consequences, but
absolutely rigorous in its development, and Sade never stops
repeating that once we begin to pay the slightest bit of attention, we cannot help but be convinced. In his novels, however,
this strength of conviction does not seem to be present at all, for
never in all of Sade's work do we find someone who has been
convinced by it. In fact, the interlocutors, those to whom Sade's
discourse is addressed, may be the victims, but the discourse is
addressed to them only insofar as they are victims and not at all
as true interlocutors. The true interlocutor is the other libertine
who is present, or who is absent and who—naturally—is even
more fully persuaded by this discourse in that he has already
accepted its fundamental precepts. Moreover, he himself has
proffered the same argument a few pages earlier. Therefore, the
die has already been cast. The discourse is addressed to the victim as target, but the interlocutor is the other libertine, who does
not need to be convinced. Sade's discourse, therefore, does not

really function as a means of persuasion, but as something quite different. In fact, it is addressed by one libertine to another.

Moreover, it would be highly disturbing if the victims were persuaded for they would then no longer be victims and could no longer be toyed with. Consequently, it is necessary that the victims not be persuaded, that the discourse not have a persuasive function; therefore, the discourse is addressed to other libertines. But why since they've already been convinced? I believe that this discourse serves primarily as a heraldic blazon, a sign of recognition. It is there to establish a threshold of differentiation between libertines and victims. In effect, either someone acknowledges the four arguments, the four fundamental negations, and, at that moment, is a libertine, or he fails to acknowledge all four of them or overlooks one, even one, and, given their unity, at that moment the individual is not a true libertine and can be placed alongside the other victims. Therefore, the four arguments serve as a sign, a test, a kind of examination of differentiation to determine if someone should be ranged among the victims or the libertines. It is in this form that we often find these well-known discourses, which function as a kind of evaluation. When Minski, the anthropophagous giant, meets the respectable Juliette, he asks her several questions: "Don't you believe in God?" "Of course not," Juliette responds. Having passed the exam, Minski recognizes that Juliette is a libertine, a libertine like him and, therefore, Juliette will not be raped. Of course, she will undergo various forms of violence, but she will not be murdered; she will not be eaten, and so on. Therefore, she has joined the libertines.

Then, again in the same register, a second functional variant of this general function of recognition among libertines is that libertines set traps for one another to determine if they remain at the same degree of libertinage. They set traps for one another and present one another with various tests, enacting a kind of theoretical comedy. Returning to the scene involving little Fontange, one of the last scenes in *Juliette*, we find that Juliette has encountered Noirceuil again and does not know if his attitude remains unchanged or if he is as much of a libertine as before. So she says to him, "I've just encountered little Fontange, who has been entrusted to my care along with her mother's very considerable assets; I've decided to return those assets to her and provide her with the lavish wedding I promised her mother."[2] At that moment, Noirceuil is surprised and thinks that Juliette has changed. He begins to doubt. Given this, and seeing that Noirceuil's attitude has not changed (because he is worried and even indignant to see such wholesome sentiments in her), Juliette is reassured. She realizes that Noirceuil has remained at the same degree of libertinism and, at that moment, the two libertines acknowledge each other. Neither has fallen into the trap set for the other.

The need to set traps is considerable, for we shouldn't approach these four arguments as four articles of a dogma that would be accepted once and for all, nor are they the fatal and necessary consequences of impeccable reasoning. At bottom they are moral tasks and, at any moment, even the most extreme libertine might overlook one of them given the difficulty of observing all four simultaneously while maintaining the same intensity of focus. And as it happens, during the course of Juliette's story, several libertines who had followed the four arguments suddenly overlooked one, and at that moment ceased being true libertines. There is a quite remarkable individual by the name of Cordelli, for example, who, during a highly charged scene in which he rapes, murders, cooks, and eats his daughter, gives signs of the greatest libertinism. After the scene, he withdraws to a small room. Juliette spies on him and sees that Cordelli repents for what he has done and prays to God, in the event that God might exist, to forgive him for what he has done. Cordelli has sidestepped the first argument concerning the existence of God. Therefore, he's not a good libertine; in fact, he's no longer a libertine at all and will be killed in turn. The same thing happens to Saint-Fond. He does support the four arguments for a certain period of time but eventually allows one to escape, not the argument concerning the nonexistence of God but the immortality of the soul. Saint-Fond acts as follows: At the moment when one of his victims is about to die, he brings her into one of his private chambers, where he forces her to undergo the most abominable forms of blasphemy, such that if her soul were eternally immortal, that soul would be eternally damned. And Saint-Fond says, "But what an admirable form of suffering, for if the soul were immortal, I would be certain to have caused my victim to suffer not just during her lifetime but throughout all eternity." This was, therefore, the height of suffering. To which Juliette and Clairvil remark, quite correctly, that this eternity of suffering is conceivable only if the soul is immortal, which proves that Saint-Fond has ceased to observe the argument that the soul is mortal, consequently, Saint-Fond will have to be punished. That is why he is effectively sacrificed by Noirceuil. Thus, the function of the heraldic blazon, the function of recognition, of distinction, of the ordeal, and ordeals perpetually renewed.

This function of differentiation is important, for it encompasses two series of consequences. It enables the affirmation of these arguments. Acceptance of these endlessly repeated discourses is used to discriminate between two categories of individual: those known as victims, individuals who, in a sense, fall outside the discourse, who remain external, who do not and never will allow themselves to be persuaded. These individuals will become, by the mere fact of their being external to the discourse, a kind of infinite object. That is, the libertine's desire will torment them indefinitely, will torment their body, every portion of their body, every centimeter of their anatomy, every organ. Rape, of course, is merely the first episode and the ordeal will be completed only when the activity of the Sadean character will have exerted itself upon the deepest realms of the person's anatomy, when the individual has been violated, cut into pieces, broken up, when her entrails have been torn out and her heart has been eaten, when everything that is inside the body has been removed and no single part remains intact. This is the infinite division, enacted by the desire of the other, of the body that falls outside the discourse. In other words, if you fall outside the discourse, your body will become an endless object of desire, an endless object of persecution, of sharing, of dismemberment; the body of the one who is outside the discourse is infinitely subdivided. From the moment one is outside the discourse, the body loses its unity, its sense of organization, its sovereignty; the body is no longer whole, and by that fact alone becomes the unending interaction of all the possible objects of desires that grow, multiply, and disappear in the face of the violence of the other. So, there we have the victim.

There are libertines, however, partners, those who are inside the discourse, those who accept the four arguments and remain within the confines of those four arguments. What happens to them, what happens to their bodies? First, they will not die. It is understood by the libertines that from the moment one is recognized as a libertine, those who accept the four arguments will not be killed. Yet, their body can be used, in fact, the libertine must even proffer that body, but it will be given in an entirely different form. He will offer his mouth, his sex, he'll offer whatever part of his body pleases his partner, but he will freely offer this body, a body that must be relinquished, out of a sense of organic unity. The person who uses the body of the libertine—the other libertine—must, if the need arises, offer a similar, possibly symmetrical, part of his own body. However, this division of the body is not infinite (as in the case of the victim) but organic. The libertine is, for the other libertine, inside the discourse of the four arguments; he is not an infinite object like the victim but what I'll call an "elementary" object. Therefore, this discourse allows us to distinguish infinite objects as objects of desire, to be murdered and apportioned without end, while the elementary objects will be divided, but according to an anatomy and in such a way that the integrity of the body and the integrity of life are preserved. The libertine won't die from having offered his body, whereas the victim will always die from the effect of this infinite division. So, Sadean discourse has a second function, which is this distinction between two types of erotic object: the partner, or elementary object, and the victim, or infinite object.

Here—and this is the second group of consequences—two rather difficult problems arise. According to the first function of Sadean discourse, anything that might limit desire was set aside. But now this second function, by distinguishing two types of objects, the victim and the partner, introduces a limitation, in truth, two limitations. On the one side, the victim object, the infinite object, will necessarily disappear, will die, will be end-lessly anatomized, until nothing remains of him and the moment arises when my desire for this victim will encounter the limit of disappearance. The victim will no longer be around to satisfy desire while I, on the other hand, have the right to touch the partner, in the sense that I can borrow some part of his body and, yet, do not have the right to kill him. In the [Statutes of] the Society of the Friends of Crime, Article 2 contains the fol-lowing statement: "theft is permitted within the bounds of the [Society]; but murder is not, except in the seraglios," the sera-glios being the places where the victims are kept.[3] There, mur-der is possible, but among libertines there can be no murder. And when Juliette leaves Minski's château in Italy, where she has been both a prisoner and a sovereign, someone will advise her to kill Minski, emphasizing how pleasant that would be, to which Juliette replies that, yes, that would be very agreeable, but Minski is a libertine and, consequently, she cannot kill him, she doesn't have the right. Here we encounter another limit of desire. Therefore, there are two limits: if I wish to preserve the object of my desire, I must make him my equal, but he must be a libertine; conversely, if I want the other to be a victim, if, therefore, I want to possess that person endlessly, I'll kill him and he will disappear. This problem helps to reveal the third function of Sadean discourse, which I shall call the function of destination.

In all these discourses, however, there is something highly paradoxical. The discourse appears in one or more forms, the repetition of the four assertions of nonexistence (God, the soul, crime,[4] and nature do not exist). Yet, let us assume that God does not exist. It is obvious that nothing religion can teach or proscribe exists; in which case, we have only chimeras, illusions, errors, and so on. Therefore, if God does not exist, can the libertine, convinced of this nonexistence, have any desire at all? For example, making love in a church or ejaculating on the Host? If it is true that incest, the crime of incest, does not exist, what pleasure can the libertine have in choosing to make love to a member of his family? Yet, at every moment, we see that Sade's characters experience the greatest pleasure and desire in performing acts of this nature. Here, I'm thinking very specifically of the episode with Bressac. Bressac explains to Justine that the natural ties binding the family do not exist. After all, what is a mother? Why, nothing at all! A mother is simply a woman who, one day or one night, made love to someone, who experienced pleasure, and from this purely personal pleasure, there ensued, as a consequence of a physiological process, the birth of a child. Perhaps she nourished this child, but here as well, nourishing a child is simply the satisfaction of a natural instinct or a physiological need and purely animal. The best proof is that female animals nourish their young. We could say that the maternal bond goes further than this because mothers take care of their children, provide for their education, and so on. To which Bressac responds: this is merely vanity; mothers want their children to succeed, to become wise, and so on. Therefore, if you consider the progress and development of the bond of affection between mother and child, you find no more than a succession of pleasures (physical pleasure, physiological need, the pleasure of vanity), and there is nothing, nothing, that in any way, in its specificity, establishes a maternal bond, a bond between mother and child, that would be sacred and inviolable. Having explained this, Bressac could, and should, say that, ultimately, if there are no special bonds between mother and child, making love to one's mother, or one's maid, or one's cousin, or a stranger makes no difference, other than, possibly, the beauty or youth of the person. However, it turns out that Bressac is an unregenerate homosexual and, therefore, he should say, after all, "She may be my mother, but I have no desire for her any more than for any other woman." But Bressac, specifically, notwithstanding his principled and habitual homosexuality, makes an exception—the only exception of his life—for his mother; for the fact that she's his mother creates in him such a degree of erotic excitation that he sodomizes her. Therefore, the fact that she's his mother plays a specific role in his desire. It is because she's his mother that desire is triggered and fulfilled.

We could continue this same line of thinking with respect to the pope and God. Justine, much later in the novel, meets the pope and, of course, does horrid things with this pope.[5] These horrors are preceded by a lengthy speech by the pope, who says, "You know, God doesn't exist, and I'm in a position to know!" And there, he takes Justine by the hand and leads her to the tomb of Saint Peter in the basilica of Saint Peter, where he makes love to her. But, if God truly doesn't exist, what difference does it make? It's not exactly more comfortable than other places! If rational discourse eliminates God, the soul, nature, the law (everything that must be respected in the human world), then, at bottom, doesn't the discourse eliminate those privileged objects of libertinage: insulting God, defiling nature, the affronts to human relationships, and so on?

At this stage, I believe we need to take a closer look at Sadean discourse. There are some passages, very few, that employ a kind of standard eighteenth-century discourse, a "generic" discourse, in which Sade says: "God doesn't exist; he's a product of the imagination, born long ago from the fear mankind experienced in the face of natural phenomena and then, little by little, based on that uncertainty and that initial anxiety, God's image was formed and, consequently, we don't have to respect it because it was merely due to that." This is the typical late-eighteenth-century discourse of aggressive rationalism, but it's rarely found in Sade. The great Sadean discourse is constructed quite differently, in fact, it's constructed in reverse. It does not consist in saying "God doesn't exist, therefore, he is neither good nor bad," but rather, "God is cruel and, therefore, because God is cruel and because it's a contradiction for an omnipotent, infinitely merciful God to be cruel, God cannot exist." Sade does not say, "The maternal bond does not exist; the mother is simply another person and, therefore, we shouldn't ask if she is good or bad, or if it's good or evil to make love to her." He says, "My mother experienced pleasure with my father; my mother experienced this pleasure without thinking about me, the person who was going to be born, therefore, my mother is cruel, and if she is cruel, she is not good. But, the essence of motherhood is always to be good, consequently, the mother does not exist." Therefore, it is not through the establishment or affirmation of nonexistence that Sade deduces the fact of indifference to the law and the forbidden; rather, it is from the cruelty of the objects in question that he ultimately deduces their nonexistence, which is quite different and which also presents several rather difficult logical problems.

In general terms, the framework of the argument is as follows. God is cruel; but cruelty contradicts the existence of a perfect God, defined by his omnipotence and goodness. Therefore, God cannot and must not exist. Sade's discourse amounts to saying that the greater God's cruelty, the less he will exist, and if God were good, he would exist. God, a cruel God, does not exist and if God is slightly crueler than that, he'll even exist somewhat less. The nonexistence that is deduced from cruelty increases as cruelty increases. Sade resumes the same argument in discussing nature. Sade does not say, "Nature does not exist, therefore, there is no sense in saying that it is good or bad." He says, "Nature destroys; it spends its time in creating beings but just as soon as they are created, it consigns them to death or abandonment, or they die of old age, or they are killed. In any event, nature condemns those beings to die, which is contradictory." Therefore, it is in the nature of things that a being condemned to death will turn against nature; and he does so in two ways: by killing himself or by killing another creature, in which case he is doing what nature does. Therefore, he's obeying the natural law, but he does so in place of nature, which is a way of killing nature (each time I kill someone, I take the place of nature, therefore, I kill nature). Or the individual refuses to let himself be killed. At that moment, he preserves what nature has created. He obeys the natural law. But since natural law consists in the fact that living individuals die, when a living individual refuses to die, he scorns nature because, here too, he does the contrary of what nature does. From this tissue of contradictions, all of which are the logical consequence of the cruelty of nature, we conclude that nature does not exist or, rather, that nature's existence diminishes as her cruelty increases. The greater nature's destructiveness, the less it will exist. From this type of discourse, which consists in saying, "God is cruel, therefore God does not exist and the greater his cruelty, the less he will exist; nature does not exist because nature is cruel; human relations don't exist because men are cruel"; from this type of discourse, therefore, we can draw several rather important consequences.

The first consequence is that Sade's logic is an anti-Russellian logic or, if you prefer, we can imagine Russell's logic as being the furthest from that of Sade.[6] At least one of the forms of Russellian logic states that a proposition of the type "the mountain of gold is in California" cannot be true or false unless it is broken down and we can first state that the mountain of gold exists and then that the mountain of gold is in California. Sade's reasoning is based on a logic that is the exact opposite of this because he does not say, "Nature exists and *then* nature is cruel," but "Nature is cruel, therefore, nature does not exist." It is a question of deducing from an attributive judgment a judgment of nonexistence concerning the subject of attribution, which is logically inconceivable, impracticable, and nonetheless lies at the heart of Sadean logic. This logic is absolutely foreign to Russell's logic; it is equally foreign to Cartesian logic. For, if you compare Sade's argument with Descartes's ontological argument, you see that it's exactly the opposite. For, Descartes's logic consists in saying, God is perfect, yet, perfection implies existence, therefore, the God who is perfect exists. It is a question of starting from an attributive judgment and concluding with an existential judgment. Sade is anti-Cartesian, just as he is anti-Russellian, because he starts from an attributive judgment not to deduce existence but to deduce nonexistence. To that extent, we can say that Sade's logic is rigorously monstrous because between the "intuitionist" logic of Descartes, which necessarily rests on the idea and the existence of the idea, consequently on the possible, and Russell's formalist logic, Sade has managed to construct a form of logic that is absolutely nonviable in terms of logic: starting from an attributive judgment, he reaches a judgment of the nonexistence of the very thing about which the attribution is made. So, these are the first two consequences of Sadean discourse, which functions, as we'll see below, within Western philosophy in a way that is absolutely perverse and destructive.

The third consequence is that these nonexistent monstrosities—God, others, crime, law, nature, and so on—are in no way illusions as the eighteenth century understood them. Why? Because once an illusion has been discovered, we will obviously feel free and have nothing further to do with the object discovered to be illusory. This is what eighteenth-century criticism did when it demonstrated, for example, that God did not exist or that the soul was an illusion. Once such claims had been demonstrated, we were rid of them once and for all. Sade, however, does not treat God, the soul, nature, and the law as illusions but as chimeras, and he in fact calls them "chimeras." The chimera is not something that does not exist, it is something whose existence diminishes the more it is what it is. God is a chimera in the sense that his existence diminishes the more he is equal to his essence, the closer he gets to what he is and what he must be, which is to say that his existence decreases as his cruelty increases. The more God approaches his own cruelty, the more nature approaches her own savagery, the less either of them exist. While the eighteenth century believed that an illusion was something that did not exist and should therefore be gotten rid of, the Sadean chimera is something whose existence diminishes the more it is what it is.

Finally, we have the fourth consequence: If it is true that God's existence diminishes as his cruelty increases, then what will increase his cruelty, what will make him increasingly cruel, and, consequently, lead to his diminished existence? What, then, is this cruelty? God's cruelty is one that causes men to kill other men, that causes the virtuous to be born only to become victims to the bad actions of others. What makes God cruel is that there are libertines who enable vice to triumph at the very moment when virtue is persecuted. In general, what is it that makes God increasingly cruel, what is it that augments God's cruelty other than the existence of the libertine? The greater the number of libertines, the more libertine the libertine becomes, the more God's cruelty will not only be demonstrated but effectively realized. The libertine is God's cruelty made flesh. While it is true that Christ is God's goodness incarnate, the libertine is the Christ of God's cruelty and the greater the number of libertines, the greater God's cruelty. But we have seen that as God's cruelty increases, his existence decreases; consequently, the multiplication of libertines and the profusion of libertinage will increasingly ensure the nonexistence of God and, therefore, the nonexistence of God is not a theoretical argument, affirmed once and for all as a truth that could be deduced through reason and by which we could then deduce that reasoning. God's nonexistence is something that is realized at every moment as God's cruelty, as God's cruelty enacted, in the person and in the conduct of the libertine. Thus, desire and truth, or libertine desire and the truth that God does not exist, are linked by a relation that is not at all the relation of a principle to its consequences. It's much more complex than that. Because God is cruel, libertines exist and, consequently, pitiless desires also exist, and the more libertines there are, the more desires are pitiless, and the truth that God does not exist will be all the greater. The truth that God does not exist and the multiplication of signs are, therefore, connected to one another in a kind of endless process. As we multiply our desires, we multiply our cruelty, we increasingly aggravate the pitiless character of our desires and God's existence will continue to diminish. The connection between truth and desire brings about the monstrosity of the chimera, with the result that this chimera, the chimera that is God or nature, or the law, or the soul, this chimera becomes increasingly monstrous, which is to say, increasingly chimerical, which is to say, exists less and less and, by existing less and less, becomes increasingly cruel, increasingly monstrous, and so on. And it continues in this way without God ever becoming totally silent, without God ever actually disappearing from the horizon of desire. God's nonexistence is fulfilled at every moment in Sadean discourse and desire.

Therefore, we can say that Sade's desire does not eliminate, as we might fear, the object of desire but desire and discourse struggle with each other for the same object. When I mentioned earlier that it's strange that Sade's discourses speak of God and not desire, when I made that remark, I forgot one fundamental thing, which is that Sade's discourses indeed speak of God but desire is also addressed to God, and discourse and desire effectively have the same object: God, to the extent that he does not exist and to the extent that he must be destroyed at every moment . . . And it is this connection between discourse and desire that is fundamental to Sadean discourse. Given this, it is relatively easy to deduce the last two functions of discourse in Sade's writing.

In reality, these two last functions confront the first two and, to a certain extent, limit, challenge, and dispute them. The first two functions were those of de-castration and differentiation, the recognition of libertines by other libertines and the recognition of victims as victims. In terms of these first two functions, our fourth function will challenge the second, the fifth will challenge the first, and between these four figures, we have a third function, which is the function of destruction.

The fourth function is that of rivalry: Sade's discourses are always the same. We always find the same four arguments tirelessly and endlessly repeated. But when we look a little closer, we find that those discourses vary and that they vary in different ways. They vary depending on the situation. For example, when it is a question of appropriating little Fontange's heritage, the discourse turns to the relationships among men, to the more or less sacred character of obligation, to the social contract, the sanctions enacted by society, and so on. And when, on the contrary, the discussion turns, in the person of Bressac, to desire for the mother, the discourse addresses family relationships. So, the discourse varies with the object in question; it also varies with the individuals involved, and the discourse of individuals will vary depending on their own character, their social situation, and their education.

For example, there is a discourse by a woman by the name of Dubois. Dubois is a woman of the people and her argument goes something like this: "Nature, in creating men, was not concerned with making them unequal; she made them all largely according to the same model; it is society that created inequality. Therefore, it is natural to restore equality at the expense of society. But society, being based on inequality, does not want men to be equal, we can only restore equality through violence." And she creates an entire theory of violence, of the violence needed to restore, against society, the natural equality assumed to have been established from the outset. A system such as this, which we find only in Dubois, will not be found among the aristocrats who are introduced by Sade.

There is also the papal system. The pope has a very particular system, which consists in first claiming, obviously, that God does not exist. For the pope, the only creator is nature, but nature is not good. Nature consists solely of a destructive rage, with which it is thoroughly imbued, and, therefore, mankind can do but one thing, which is to revolt against nature and, whenever a natural inclination appears in man, it is the duty of the libertine to reject this natural inclination and do something other than what nature dictates. In this way, because nature is bad, man will scorn nature, rebel against it; for example, he will refuse to have children by systematically practicing sodomy. What then will happen? If man only engages in sodomy, humanity will ultimately be destroyed and humanity will disappear, which, the pope notes, is exactly what nature desires, for nature demands only one thing, which is that humanity should disappear—the best proof being that nature is utterly cruel toward humanity. We see how this system is very exactly adapted to the pope, precisely to the pope. For the pope does not preach about God but about nature, not about universal goodness but about universal cruelty, not about salvation and the propagation of individual beings but of their destruction, not about the eternity of humanity but its ultimate disappearance, and so all the traditional functions of the pope are reversed within his discourse.

There is also the strange system of Saint-Fond and several other systems, which differ somewhat among themselves. As a result, when we examine the grain of such discourse, when we move from the four generally accepted arguments to the implementation of those four arguments and the way in which they are explicated, we see that each libertine has his own way of connecting them. Each libertine has his own way of demonstrating how those arguments are organized, what they are based on, how they can be justified, the consequences that can be drawn, and the criminal or sexual practices that can be deduced from them. This means that there is no general Sadean system, there is no one Sadean philosophy, there is no Sadean materialism, no Sadean atheism. There exists a plurality of systems that are juxtaposed and that communicate with one another only through the network of the four arguments we discussed earlier.

This network, those four elements, can be used, like different crystals, to construct discourses that are absolutely specific to a situation or an individual, and Sade does indeed refer to the various physiognomies assumed by these four arguments as a "system." We frequently find one character saying to another, "Tell me about your system, explain your system to me. Why have you done what you did? Describe your system, and so on." And this system will be the crystallization, specific to a situation and an individual, of the four arguments I spoke of earlier. Consequently, and this explains how this fourth function of discourse contrasts with the second, the Sadean discourses (in addition to the fact that they have a function of recognition and sharing between libertines and victims) give rise to another function. This consists in distinguishing—even among libertines—individuals who cannot be reduced to one another, individuals who are characterized by their system, because the systems differ from individual to individual. Thus, there is no general system of libertinage, but for each libertine there is a system, and those systems define the singularity, or what Sade calls the irregularity of individuals. Every individual is irregular and his own irregularity is manifested, is symbolized, in his system. But those systems, to the extent that they are different, to the extent that they will shatter this unified world of libertinism that appeared to arise from the second function, to the extent that they will shatter a world that is continuous, complicit, and collaborative with libertinism, ensure that Sade's libertines cannot be substituted for one another, cannot replace one another, and remain isolated from one another.

Libertines, therefore, have systems of varying strength and, depending on the strength of the system, the libertine might be vanquished or, on the contrary, triumph over other libertines. The systems appear as instruments among libertines and, with that we see, in this more granular operation of Sadean discourse, how the reputed liberty of libertines, which was limited as we saw earlier, since they did not have the right to kill one another, we see how this obligation disappears and how libertines, unlike wolves, devour one another. A libertine may kill another libertine and may do so whenever his argument is stronger than the other's. We find a good example of this when Clairvil and Juliette decide to kill Borghese. Both of them had found a willing accomplice, a willing partner in libertinage in the Princess Borghese. But it turns out that her philosophical argument is weaker than that of Clairvil and Juliette. Because of the weakness of her philosophical argument, Princess Borghese believes that the relationships established among the three libertines are sacred and cannot be challenged. Consequently, her conviction in the argument by which crime does not exist and everything is possible is not total. She has admitted that one crime is possible, namely, killing a companion in libertinism, and, therefore, she hesitates in taking the step to commit such a crime. Which means that her system is going to be weaker because of this than the system of Clairvil and Juliette, and it is precisely by attacking the weakest link in the system that Clairvil and Juliette will attack Borghese and set a trap for her. Borghese, who does not believe the bonds of libertinism can be broken, does not see the trap and falls into it, and it is the weakness of her system that allows the others to kill her. The law stating that libertines cannot attack one another and cannot kill one another does not hold when things are taken to their ultimate conclusion. For, while it's true that the four arguments enable libertines to recognize one another and put themselves, with respect to desire, in a very different position than their victims, nonetheless, the difference between the systems constructed on the basis of those four arguments results in an incessant struggle among them, an infinite struggle that, in the end, will result in the survival of only one of them: Juliette. And in this way Juliette will sacrifice all her companions in libertinism: Clairvil, Saint-Fond, la Borghese, of course, all of them will be destroyed. There remains only Juliette, flanked, for reasons that have to do purely with libertinism, by Noirceuil, on one hand, and Madame Durand, on the other, who becomes her servant. So much for the fourth role of Sadean discourse. The fifth role is very easily deduced.

The fifth function of Sadean discourse is as follows. If it's true that the discourse we had initially believed distinguished libertines from victims also distinguished libertines from one another, and if it's true that this discourse serves not only as a heraldic blazon for all libertines when confronting their victims but as an instrument of combat among libertines themselves, then the discourse can expose the libertine to death. By comparing his discourse to that of others, the libertine may risk death; moreover, not only would he risk death, but he must, if he pushes his argument to its extreme, acknowledge that he too may be touched by death, in fact, that death is the most wonderful thing that could happen to him. If it's true that nature does not exist, that the soul is not immortal, that God does not exist, and that there is no such thing as true crime, then what does it mean for someone, even a libertine, to die? Isn't this the greatest offense against nature—to give oneself up, to accept death? For nature has created us, but no sooner have we been created than it abandons us, leaving us with nothing more than the need to survive, the only trace, in a way, of the gesture it made in creating us. From that moment on, when we renounce the need to survive and turn the need to survive into the need to die, we turn against nature, we scorn nature, we commit against ourselves the greatest crime imaginable, and at that moment, it is obvious that it is also the greatest pleasure. Consequently, we achieve the greatest sexual excitement at the moment of our acceptance of death, and it is in this way that all of Sade's great libertines, who, nonetheless, do all they can not to die, accept death when they must. Bressac is prepared, he says, to bear witness to the [. . .] to the point of martyrdom.[7] He admits that if he were to encounter someone stronger than himself, he would allow that stronger man to dispose of him, even if it meant his death. Princess Borghese says that she would be happy on the scaffold and, therefore, when she is thrown into the volcano by Clairvil and Juliette, we have to assume that in the very destruction of her body upon the rocks, she will attain the highest degree of pleasure. Juliette says, "There is nothing I fear less in this world than the noose. Is it not common knowledge that death upon the gallows is accompanied by a discharge? And discharging is something that will never hold terrors for me. If ever a judge sends me to the scaffold, you will see me come forward with light and impudent step."[8] And Madame Durand says, "One cannot doubt that death, as required by nature, must become pleasurable, for we have convincing proof that all of life's needs are merely pleasures." There is another astonishing character in the novel, a Swedish woman, who asks her lover to put her to death. Obviously, he doesn't hesitate because she asks that he do so, and if he were to hesitate it would be out of fear, fear on the part of the one who wants to see her suffer, that she might experience too much pleasure in dying. He appeases his scruples, however, and kills her. And at that moment, in this fifth function, we rediscover, in an inverted form, what we found in the first function, which assured the individual that there was absolutely no limit to his desire, that he would in a sense be entirely de-castrated, that the entire universe would be incorporated into the circuit of his narcissism, that nothing of himself would ever be sacrificed. The first function of discourse ensured the individual that no one would any longer say to him "you'll remain yourself if you renounce this or that." The fifth argument, however, states that "the greatest pleasure you will encounter in life will occur on the day your very individuality disappears," and it is here that we find the contrast between the fifth argument and the first.

We now have the complete edifice of the functions of Sadean discourse, all of them centered around this third function I refer to as "destructive," which is constructed with the de-castrating function. This is juxtaposed to the function of the self-suppression of the individual, and the function of recognition or differentiation, which is juxtaposed to the function of struggle, rivalry, and combat. At the same time, we see how the analysis of these four functions can be used to isolate the concepts I believe are fundamental in Sade: the function of de-castration, which is used to very precisely define what we call a libertine; the function of differentiation, which is used to define what we call a victim; the destructive function, which is used to define what Sade calls a chimera; the function of rivalry, or struggle, which is used to define what Sade called systems; and, finally, the last function, which is used to define the individual or, rather, to define how the individual himself is nothing at all, so that, to the four fundamental arguments we began with, we should add, as a result of this fifth function, a fifth argument: the individual himself does not exist.

To conclude, I would simply say that we need to very carefully avoid imposing on Sade two models of reading. First of all, the Freudian model. It's important to understand that it is not at all the role of Sadean discourse to express the truth about desire. Sade is not seeking to introduce an analysis or explication of sexual desire or sexuality. In Sade, desire is not the subject of reasonable discourse; in fact, true discourse and desire exist on the same plane, are profoundly interrelated. True discourse multiplies desire, deepens it, makes it infinite, just as desire makes discourse all the more true. Therefore, there is no level of desire on which a level of discourse might be superimposed, a level of nature and then a truth that would clarify that nature. In fact, discourse and desire are interlinked and engaged with each other, they are not subordinate to each other. They are arranged in an order that is, in truth, disorder itself. And to that extent, I do not believe that we can compare Sadean discourse and Freudian discourse. Whether the function and role of Freudian discourse is to speak the truth about desire, whether Freud wanted to express a natural, psychological, or philosophical truth matters little; if his intention was to express the truth about desire, then, Freudian discourse and Sadean discourse are strictly incompatible. The only possible objection would be to claim that the role of psychoanalysis was not to expose, and Freud did not wish to express, the truth about desire; or that Freud may not have wanted to associate desire with truth. Maybe the role of the psychoanalytic cure, the role of discourse in the field of psychoanalysis, may not be to associate desire with a world of truth but to rearticulate the fundamental relationship between desire and truth. Maybe it's a question, as part of the psychoanalytic cure, of restoring the desiring function of truth and the truth function of desire. In that case, it's not Freud who can help us read Sade but Sade who can help us read Freud, because this is precisely what Sade does in his text. He did not want to elevate a desire that the West had given over to lies, illusion, and ignorance, to the light of truth;

that's not at all what he was trying to do. He wanted to restore the desiring function of truth; he wanted to show the truth function of desire; he wanted to show that truth and desire are like two faces of the same ribbon, winding endlessly around itself. So, we shouldn't read Sade in terms of this kind of traditional Freudian approach. We shouldn't say: in the West no one has ever known desire and then Sade arrived to give us a number of truths about desire, and then Freud arrived after Sade and expressed other truths. No, Sade does not express the truth about desire; he rearticulates truth and desire in terms of each other.

The second model we must avoid if we are to understand Sade is the Marcusian model. Very roughly, we can say that for Marcuse, a true discourse can free desire of its shackles.[9] Marcusian man is the man who says: what I have been doing until now with a feeling of guilt I now know that all of that was innocent and, once my illusions have dissipated, I'll be able to act innocently, that is, happily, whereas before I acted culpably. Or, I can (and this is ultimately preferable as far as Marcuse is concerned) simply not do it at all because the pleasure of punishing myself through guilt no longer exists. Therefore, everything I do will be done in complete innocence or I'll do nothing. There are some things I no longer do because I no longer experience the pleasure of feeling guilty, and I do other things innocently, without guilt, which is to say, joyfully. Sadean man, however, says nothing of the kind. He doesn't say: free us from all the shackles that limit and alienate desire. Sadean man says: I know I should have no remorse but a great danger lies ahead of me. For, if I no longer experience remorse, will I still experience pleasure in committing crime? If I no longer feel remorse, will the crime still exist sufficiently so that I experience the extremes of pleasure when committing it? I must then continue to experience the height of pleasure in the most abominable crimes. And therefore, for Sade, unlike Marcuse, the connection between truth and desire is not based on a rediscovered innocence or the absence of guilt; in fact, it does not occur at all in the state finally attained. For Sade, the connection between the truth of desire and truth comes about only in the pursuit of crime and permanent disorder.

I think it is through this relation to Sade's thought and on this basis that we should understand Freud and Marcuse and restore their relationship to each other rather than impose the Freudian or Marcusian model on Sade's text. Sade has effectively freed desire from the subordination to truth, in which it had always been subsumed in our civilization. It was Sade who, for the great Platonic edifice that yoked desire to the sovereignty of truth, substituted a relationship in which desire and truth confront each other, face each other, and struggle together within the same spiral. It was Sade who freed desire from truth. This does not mean that Sade claimed that truth had no importance for desire. Rather, he felt that desire and truth were neither subordinate to each other nor separable from each other. It was Sade who said: "Desire is unlimited only in truth and truth is active only in desire." This does not mean that desire and truth will merge into an authoritative figure in the form of happiness or a newly rediscovered peace. Rather, desire and truth are endlessly multiplied in the unfolding, the scintillation, the infinite continuation of desire.

Editors' Notes

Editors' Introduction

1 "La Fête de l'écriture," interview with J. Almira and J. Le Marchand," *Le Quotidien de Paris,* no. 328, April 25, 1975, 13; published in *Dits et écrits,* ed. Daniel Defert, François Ewald, and Jean Lagrange (Paris: Gallimard, 1995), vol. 2, text no. 154.

2 Jacques Almira, with a degree in philosophy and literature, is the author of a number of novels and short stories. He received the Prix Médicis in 1975 for *Le voyage à Naucratis* (Paris: Gallimard, 1975).

3 Jean Demelier, writer and painter, was born in Poitiers in 1940. He was a friend of Samuel Beckett and Pierre Klossowski. He gained critical recognition with the publication of his first two novels, *Le rêve de Job* (Paris: Gallimard, 1971) and *Le sourire de Jonas* (Paris: Gallimard, 1975).

4 See "Truth, Power, Self: An Interview with Michel Foucault," in P. H. Hutton, H. Gutman, and L. H. Martin, eds., *Technologies of the Self: A Seminar with Michel Foucault* (Amherst: University of Massachusetts Press, 1988), 9–15.

5 Denys Foucault, quoted in Philippe Artières, Jean-François Bert, Frédéric Gros, and Judith Revel, eds., *Cahier Foucault* (Paris: L'Herne, 2011).

6 Librarian at the ENS on the Rue d'Ulm and brother of the composer Pierre Boulez.

7 Based on documents held in the archives of the Alliance Française, available at the Uppsala University library.

8 Daniel Defert, "Chronologie," in *Dits et écrits,* vol. 1, 43.

9 Arlette Farge and Michel Foucault, *Le désordre des familles:*

Lettres de cachet des archives de la Bastille (Paris: Gallimard "Archives," 1982).

10 Michel Foucault, "The Lives of Infamous Men," in *Power: Essential Works of Foucault, 1954–1984*, vol. 3 (New York: New Press, 2001), 173.

11 Michel Foucault, "An Interview with Michel Foucault by Charles Ruas," in *Death and the Labyrinth*, with an introduction by James Faubion and a postscript by John Ashberry, trans. Charles Ruas (New York: Continuum Collection, 1986), 173.

12 Michel Foucault, *Raymond Roussel* (Paris, Gallimard, 1963), published in English as *Death and the Labyrinth*.

13 Michel Foucault, "Speaking and Seeing in Raymond Roussel," in *Aesthetics, Method, and Epistemology—Essential Works of Foucault, 1954–1984*, vol. 2 (New York: New Press, 1999), 27; our emphasis.

14 Louis Wolfson, an American writer born in 1931, was diagnosed as schizophrenic early on. His text *Le schizo et les langues*, which was written in French, was published in 1970 by Gallimard, with a preface by Gilles Deleuze. It received considerable critical acclaim, as evidenced by Foucault's text "Sept propos sur le septième ange" (in *Dits et écrits*, vol. 2, text no. 73, 13–25).

15 Jean-Pierre Brisset (1837–1919) was a pastry chef, grammarian, writer, inventor, a security guard at the railway station of Angers, elected "prince of thinkers," and made a saint of the pataphysical calendar. The pataphysical calendar was created by the College of Pataphysics. The term "pataphysics" itself was coined by the French writer Alfred Jarry, who defined it as "the science of imaginary solutions." Since its inception, it has had numerous proponents. André Breton, Jules Romains, Raymond Queneau, and Michel Foucault were attentive readers of his work. Michel Foucault republished *La grammaire logique* (Paris: Tchou, 1970) and provided an introduction, "Sept propos sur le septième ange" (in *Dits et écrits*).

Language and Madness

1 Pierre Janet described Roussel's case under the name Martial in *De l'angoisse à l'extase*. Martial was the name of the main character in *Locus Solus*, the play and later the novel of the same name by Raymond Roussel. Pierre Janet, *De l'angoisse à l'extase. Études sur les croyances et les sentiments*, vol. 1: *Un délire religieux*; *La croyance*, vol. 2: *Les sentiments fondamentaux* (Paris: Alcan, 1926, 1928).

The Silence of the Mad

1 [No reference provided in the French.—Trans.]
2 William Shakespeare, *King Lear*, act 3, scene 2 (New York: Grosset & Dunlap, 1909).
3 Miguel de Cervantes, *Don Quixote*, trans. Edith Grossman (New York: Ecco Press, 2005), 934–39.
4 [The Hôpital Général de Paris was not what we would commonly think of as a medical establishment intended to care for the sick. It was more akin to the "poorhouse," a place where the indigent or those without visible means of support were kept. In spite of its name, the "hospital" was part of the city's attempt to curb the widespread poverty of the time rather than provide medical care, and its methods were punitive rather than restorative. In fact, this was not a unique structure but a system of hospitals that included Notre Dame de la Pitié, La Salpêtrière, the Hospice de Bicêtre, and the Hospice de Vaugirard.—Trans.]
5 Denis Diderot, *Rameau's Nephew*, trans. Margaret Mauldon (London: Oxford World Classics, 2006), 67–69.
6 Antonin Artaud, *Collected Works*, vol. 1, trans. Victor Corti (London: Calder and Boyars, 1968), 27–39.
7 Mario Ruspoli (1925–86) was an Italian director, documentarian, photographer, and writer, who worked primarily in France. In 1962 he released *Regard sur la folie*, a film based on his frequent visits to the psychiatric hospital of Saint-Alban in Lozère, France.

Mad Language

1 Michel Leiris, *Rules of the Game*, vol. 1: *Scratches*, trans. Lydia Davis (Baltimore: Johns Hopkins University Press, 1997), 29–30.

2 Pierre Antoine Augustin de Piis, *L'harmonie initiative de la langue française* (Paris: L'Imprimerie de Ph.-D. Pierres, 1785).

3 Concerning Jean-Pierre Brisset, see Michel Foucault, "Sept propos sur le septième ange," in *Dits et écrits*, ed. Daniel Defert, François Ewald, and Jean Lagrange (Paris: Gallimard, 1995), vol. 2, text no. 73, 13–25.

4 Jean-Pierre Brisset, *La science de Dieu, ou la création de l'homme*, in *Œuvres completes*, ed. and with a preface by Marc Décime (Dijon: Les Presses du Réel, "L'Écart absolue"), 2001.

5 Jean Tardieu, *La Comédie du langage*, "Un mot pour un autre" [1951], in *Œuvres* (Paris: Gallimard, "Quarto" collection, 2003).

6 Michel Leiris, *Bagatelles végétales*, 1956, reprinted in *Mots sans mémoire* (Paris: Gallimard, 1998), 119–31.

7 [Postscript of the letter from Antonin Artaud to Jacques Rivière on January 29, 1924. This sentence does not appear in the Corti translation of the *Collected Works*.—Trans.]

Literature and Language: Session 1

1 Foucault's typescript is illegible at this point in the text; we refer here to the manuscript version.

2 Jean-François de la Harpe (1739–1803), writer, dramatist, and French critic born in Switzerland, highly erudite and strongly anticlerical.

3 Foucault's typescript is illegible at this point in the text; we refer here to the manuscript version.

4 Dostoevsky, in his novella *The Double*, explores this theme, which was so important to Foucault that he used a lengthy excerpt from the book for his radio presentation "Le corps et ses doubles," broadcast on January 28, 1963, as part of the program "The Use of Speech," produced by Jean Doat.

5 [This passage is a paraphrase by Foucault and does not appear in Diderot's French text.—Trans.]

6 Foucault's draft reads "nested narratives."

Literature and Language: Session 2

1 Charles-Augustin Sainte-Beuve (1804–69) was a literary critic celebrated for approaching the literary work through the prism of the author's biography. It was in opposition to Sainte-Beuve's formalized method that Proust wrote *Contre Sainte-Beuve*. For Proust, if any insight was to be gained, it was the work that would enlighten us about the life of the author and not the reverse. See *Against Sainte-Beuve and Other Essays*, trans. with an introduction and notes by John Sturrock (London: Penguin Books, 1994). [Jean-François de la Harpe (1739–1803) was a French literary critic and playwright.—Trans.]

2 Roman Jakobson (1896–1982), a Russian linguist and reader of Ferdinand de Saussure, expanded the scope of linguistics considerably by making it the framework of structuralism.

3 Foucault's draft manuscript reads as follows: "The difference between any utterance whatsoever ('Yesterday, I went to bed early') and the sentence 'For a long time, I went to bed early' is not that the second is more beautiful or more ornate; it's that, at the moment it was pronounced, a certain risk was taken obscurely (concealed from view), which means that an utterance that begins in this way might not obey the linguistic code."

4 Jean Starobinski, philosopher and literary historian (born in Geneva in 1920), is the author of many books. At the time of Foucault's presentation, he had already published *Jean-Jacques Rousseau: Transparency and Obstruction* (trans. Arthur Gold-hammer with an introduction by Robert J. Morrissey [Chicago: University of Chicago Press, 1988]); his work on Ferdinand de Saussure's research on anagrams helped strengthen the link between literary analysis and structural linguistics.

5 Georges Dumézil (1898–1986) was a French linguist and

polyglot who, in *Mythe et épopée* (1968), his major work, provided a comparative analysis of Indo-European religions and myths, within which he identified shared narrative structures.

6 Ferdinand de Saussure (1857–1913) was a Swiss linguist and the founder of modern linguistics. His *Course on General Linguistics,* published after his death, had an impact on all later linguistics as well as various social sciences (ethnology, philosophy, literary analysis) and helped establish the foundations of structuralism. See *Course on General Linguistics,* trans. Roy Harris (La Salle, Ill.: Open Court Classics, 1995).

7 Jean Starobinski, "Les anagrames de Ferdinand de Saussure," *Mercure de France,* February 1964.

8 This passage is illegible both in the typescript of the lecture and in the draft manuscript.

9 Johann Gottfried von Herder (1744–1803) was a German poet, theologian, and philosopher. He maintained a theoretical opposition to the humanism of the Enlightenment, which he felt to be abstract. His vision of history is one of continuity, every "national epoch" being sufficient unto itself. In this sense, he developed a philosophy that was quite different from that of Hegel, who postulated the development of reason in history.

10 [The original passage reads as follows:

"When she had made an End of speaking, she handed to us Letters closed and sealed; and after we had returned undying Thanks, she caused us to go forth by a Gate adjoining the transparent Chapel, where Bacbuc summoned them to propose Questions twice as high as Mount Olympus;

And so we passed through a Country full of all Delights,
  more pleasant and temperate than Tempè in Thessaly,
  more salubrious than that part of Egype which faces
    Libya,
  more irriguous and verdant than Themischyra,
  more fertile than that part of Mount Taurus which has
    a Northern Aspect,
  more so than the Hyperborean Island in the Jewish Sea,
  more so than Caligès on Mons Caspius,

scented, smiling and pleasant as is the Country of
   Touraine;
and at last we found our Ships in the Harbour."
François Rabelais, *The Five Books and Minor Writings*, a new
translation with notes by W. F. Smith (London: Alexander P.
Watt, 1893), Book V, Chapter XLVIII, 456.—Trans.]

11 Georges Poulet (1902–91) was a Belgian literary critic who
    was part of the Geneva Group that included Jean-Pierre Rich-
    ard, Jean Starobinski, and Jean Rousset. Poulet, rejecting the
    formalist approach to contemporary criticism, wrote *Stud-
    ies in Human Time,* trans. Elliott Coleman (Baltimore: Johns
    Hopkins University Press, 1956), and *The Metamorphoses of
    the Circle,* trans. Carley Dawson and Elliott Coleman in col-
    laboration with the author (Baltimore: Johns Hopkins Uni-
    versity Press, 1967), to which Foucault here makes reference.

12 Jean Starobinski, *Jean-Jacques Rousseau: Transparency and
    Obstruction,* trans. Arthur Goldhammer, with an introduc-
    tion by Robert J. Morrissey (Chicago: University of Chicago
    Press, 1988).

13 Jean Rousset (1910–2002) was a Swiss literary critic who spe-
    cialized in baroque poetry and literature. The work cited
    is *Forme et signification. Essai sur les structures littéraires, de
    Corneille à Claudel* (Paris: José Corti, 1962).

14 The manuscript continues as follows: "It is the space of those
    Mallarméan objects, par excellence, the wing and the fan:
    when open they hide from life, they conceal, they provide
    security and remoteness; but in another sense, they reveal,
    they reveal the unfurled richness of their treasure."

15 Jean-Pierre Richard (born 1922) is a writer and critic. A spe-
    cialist in the nineteenth and twentieth centuries, he has
    worked to expose the connection between language and our
    intimate relationship with the world of the senses. Here, Fou-
    cault is making reference to Richard's book on Stéphane Mal-
    larmé, *L'univers imaginaire de Mallarmé* (Paris: Éditions du
    Seuil, 1961), which Foucault discusses in *Dits et écrits,* vol. 1,
    text 28.

Lectures on Sade

1 We have identified three documents devoted to the analysis of *Justine*. The first, 14 pages long, is titled "Buffalo 1970," the second, 47 pages, is titled "Montréal, Spring 1971," and a third, of 22 pages, is titled "Oct. '72."

2 Michel Foucault, "Sade, Sergeant of Sex," in *Essential Works of Foucault, 1954–1984*, vol. 2: *Aesthetics, Method, and Epistemology* (New York: New Press, 1998).

Lectures on Sade: Session 1

1 *Aline et Valcour, ou le Roman philosophique* is an epistolary novel published in 1793.

2 Marquis de Sade, *Œuvres complètes*, vol. 4 (Paris: Jean-Jacques Pauvert, 1947–72), 56–57. See *Juliette*, trans. Austryn Wainhouse (New York: Grove Press, 1994), 640–41.

3 "Reflections on the Novel," trans. Austryn Wainhouse and Richard Seaver, in Marquis de Sade, *The 120 Days of Sodom and Other Writings* (New York: Grove Press, 1994), 111.

4 Ibid., 112.

5 *Juliette*, 1193.

Lectures on Sade: Session 2

1 That is, *La Nouvelle Justine*.

2 [This is a paraphrase of Sade's text. See *Juliette*, trans. Austryn Wainhouse (New York: Grove Press, 1994), 1153–54.—Trans.]

3 [In Sade's text this is Article 32. See ibid., 424.—Trans.]

4 Earlier, Foucault referred to this as the nonexistence of the law.

5 [It is Juliette who encounters the pope in the basilica.—Trans.]

6 Bertrand Russell (1872–1970) was a British logician, epistemologist, and politician. A mathematician by training, the author of the *Principia Mathematica* worked on the axioms and foundations of logic. The resulting philosophy is referred

to as "scientific" because it takes as its objective the application of logical analysis to classical philosophical problems, such as knowledge or the nature of mind. Russell is considered to be the founder of analytic philosophy.

7 The passage is illegible both in the typescript for the lecture and in the draft manuscript.

8 [See *Juliette*, 1014—Trans.]

9 Herbert Marcuse (1898–1979) was a German-born American philosopher and a member of the Frankfurt School. Highly influenced by Hegel, Freud, and Husserl, Marcuse identified the repressive language used in defending the reality principle and promoted an emancipated vision of mankind.

Michel Foucault (1926–1984) was a French historian and philosopher associated with the structuralist and poststructuralist movements. He is considered one of the most influential social theorists of the second half of the twentieth century in philosophy as well as in the humanities and social sciences. Among his most notable books are *Madness and Civilization, Discipline and Punish,* and *The History of Sexuality.* The University of Minnesota Press published his *Speech Begins after Death* in 2013.

Robert Bononno is a translator based in New York City. His translations include Foucault's *Speech Begins after Death* (Minnesota, 2013), *Cosmopolitics I and II* by Isabelle Stengers (Minnesota, 2010 and 2011), and *The Singular Objects of Architecture* by Jean Baudrillard and Jean Nouvel (Minnesota, 2005).

Philippe Artières is a historian at Le Centre national de la recherche scientifique in Paris. He is president of Centre Michel Foucault.

Jean-François Bert is a sociologist and historian of social sciences at Université de Lausanne in Switzerland.

Mathieu Potte-Bonneville is a philosopher at École Normale Supérieure in Lyon, France.

Judith Revel is a philosopher and Italianist at Université Paris 1 Panthéon-Sorbonne.